PRINCIPLES
OF
THEOSOPHY

PRINCIPLES OF THEOSOPHY

BY

THÉODORE MAINAGE

TRANSLATED BY
SUZANNE DUCHÉ AND YVONNE COOPER

SHEED & WARD
LONDON

B. HERDER BOOK CO.
15 & 17 SOUTH BROADWAY,
ST. LOUIS, Mo.

Nihil Obstat
    GEORGIUS D. SMITH, S.T.D.
                            Censor Deputatus

Imprimatur
    EDM. CAN. SURMONT
                          Vic. Gen.

Westmonasterii
    die 17 *Februarii*, 1927

PRINTED IN GREAT BRITAIN

CONTENTS

INTRODUCTION 9

FIRST PART: THE THEOSOPHICAL DOCTRINE

I STUDY OF OCCULT SCIENCE 13

Spiritism and Theosophy: Differences and Similitudes—Different Ways of Approaching Theosophy: Its History, Its Sources, Its Chances—The Intellectual and Doctrinal Point of View—Is Occult Science comprehensible—Theosophy and the Rights of Reason.

II FROM THE " ONE " TO VISHNU 37

The One Existence—Apparition of the " Centre of Consciousness," Ishvara, Logos or God—Maya, the Kosmic Memory—Life, Consciousness and Vibration—The Trimûrti—Origin of Matter—The Three Gûnas—Definition and rôle of the Three Logoi—The Work of Brahma—Organization of the Seven Planes and the Forty-nine Sub-Planes of the Universe—Names and Characteristics of the Great Kosmic Regions—The General Laws of Evolution—The Work of Vishnu—Forms and Form-Monads—The " Elementals " their Functions and Their Tendencies—Evolution of Life and Forms—The Devas.

III MAHADEVA 79

Man is not an Evolved Animal—The Human Monad, Work of Mahadeva—Fusion of the Monad of Form and the Human Monad—Pre-existence of the " Souls "—Fundamental Character of the Human Monad—Self-consciousness—Rupa and Arupa Worlds—Involution of the Soul—The Three Stages of Human Evolution—Development of the Mind—" Individuality " and " Personality "—The Four Stages of the Evolution of the " Thinker "—Man and his " Bodies "—The Mechanism of Reincarnation—The Development of " Love "—The Development of " Pure " Existence—Planetary Rounds and Human Races—The End of a World.

CONTENTS

SECOND PART

CRITICISM OF THE THEOSOPHICAL DOCTRINE

IV THE GOD OF THEOSOPHISTS 115

Theosophy is a Pantheistic Doctrine—The Pantheism of Occult Doctrine is Composite—It is at the same time, Idealistic, Animistic, Emanatistic, and Materialistic—The Fusion of those different Elements leads to Incoherence—Why Pantheism is a Philosophical Error—How Mrs. Annie Besant Tries to Solve the Contradiction of a Limited Infinite.

V THEOSOPHICAL EVOLUTIONISM 141

The Vibration, Essential Factor of Evolution—Superficial and Insufficient Character of that Explanation—Theosophy, Materialist System : All is Matter, and the Human Monad Possesses no Attribute, no Faculty, no Operation which may Elevate it Above Matter—The Mechanism of Evolution, as Theosophists understand and describe it, does not iunction.

VI REINCARNATION 168

Reincarnation, Great Object of Theosophical Vulgarisation—Its Narrow Relation to the Principles of the System Deprives it of all Philosophical Basis—Reincarnation and Experimental Reality : The Problem of Human Inequalities—The Doctrine of Reincarnation is an Unverifiable Hypothesis—It does not Explain, from a Moral Point of View, the Inequalities—It Justifies the short-comings of Human Nature—It multiplies pain without necessity—What Christians Profess Touching Divine Justice.

VII THEOSOPHY AND RELIGIONS 200

Attitude of Theosophists Towards Religion—Theosophy, Source and Term of all Religions—Why this Pretention is not Justified—As a Matter of Fact, Theosophy is, Pre-eminently, the Destructive Agent of all Religion—Why it Cannot, Itself, Claim the Title of Religion—Theosophy and Christianity.

CONTENTS 7

VIII THEORY OF KNOWLEDGE 225

    Peculiar Character of Theosophical " Knowledge "—
The Two Stages of " Knowledge "—Knowledge " By
Images "—The Illusion—The Power of Thought—
How the Adept Escapes Danger—" Intuitive " Knowledge ; Its Term ; The Inner Vision of the Universal
Self—The Last Word of Human Destiny, According to
Theosophy—Conclusion.

INTRODUCTION

This book is the expression of a sincere and impartial effort to understand and judge the doctrine known under the name of Theosophy. The favour with which this doctrine has been received is evidence that the time is well chosen to undertake such a study. Last July, the Theosophical Society celebrated, in Paris, its first " World Congress." The sittings of that Congress, held in the Temple of the Square Rapp, were concluded by a much-talked-of lecture, given, in the great Sorbonne amphitheatre, by Mrs. Besant herself, the rector of the Paris University being present, together with the highest Parisian personalities. And, while her hearers loudly cheered Mrs. Besant, the press undertook to re-echo the enthusiasm of this Parisian audience throughout France by a real concert of articles.

Only ten years ago, such a manifestation would have been impossible. It shows the progress that Theosophical ideas have made.

We have just used the word " favour "; perhaps we should say " craze." For, when, for several months, one has been trying to grasp a system which claims to be the last word of human thought, one has some right to wonder whether many of the people who call themselves Theosophists know exactly what they believe when they give themselves that name.

Of course, we shall not insult the true adepts in the doctrine by supposing that they are ignorant, or semi-ignorant. They, we do not doubt, know not only the outer form, but the basis and principles of the occult science. But there is round them a considerable number of people who are attracted by it and are drawn into it by a superficial view of things.

Theosophy, like its rival, Spiritism, has benefited from the painful events which have just shaken the world. The need for religion, more or less sent to sleep by the chloroform of modern rationalism, has been suddenly awakened by the hard realities of war. Many souls, who had forgotten the faith of their childhood, or who had never had any faith at all, have cast an anxious look beyond this world. On the ocean of incredulity and scepticism, they have sought to grasp any straw. Theosophy came their way, they clung to it. Is it not striking to see that the theses which most appeal to the public are precisely those which are considered most able to pour a soothing balm on incurable or badly healed wounds? Those theses are survival, reincarnation, and successive lives.

Now—and on this point we are not afraid of being contradicted by those who know—one is not a Theosophist because one admits, more or less vaguely, the idea of survival or of reincarnation. One is really and fully a Theosophist if one has gone to the very end of Theosophical thought, and professes much more than survival and reincarnation.

To enlighten these souls, lingering on the threshold of the Temple, who think and call themselves Theosophists, but who are not, or are only half Theosophists; to enlighten also other people impressed by the intensive propaganda organised for the benefit of the new gospel, we have undertaken a somewhat difficult study, the result of which we submit to our readers. Before taking the final step which would make us, properly and fully speaking, Theosophists, it is only right to know where we are being

INTRODUCTION

led. After that, every man can judge for himself. Roman Catholics especially, will be able to decide if they can possibly harmonise their Christian faith with the faith of Mrs. Annie Besant.

As a matter of fact, the inquiry consists almost exclusively of an investigation into the thought of the well-known president and that of her fellow-workers. We are aware that there are other interpretations of the Theosophical doctrine. They all have the same value, and all borrow from the same source of pantheistic ideas. So we have found it better to concentrate our attention on one of them, which happens to be, by the way, the best known in our country.

Our work includes two different parts. Before criticizing the system, it seems only fair to show its broad outlines. This objective description, founded on texts, will allow people who do not know enough about the matter to form a general idea of the object of our discussion. It may be useful for that purpose. We have tried to make it as clear as possible. If, here and there, it appears somewhat obscure, the author of that summary admits no responsibility with regard to Theosophists. It is not his fault if the disciples of the Mahatmas enjoy speaking nonsensically, in a manner which agrees little with the clear genius of the French language. As a matter of fact—the reader will realise this when reading the second part of the book—that obscurity in words hides a background of very common ideas, easy to recognise under their majestic disguise.

Nevertheless, a study of this kind is bound to have a rather austere aspect. The reader, to follow it to the end, will have to forearm himself with a large provision of patience and good will. He will often have the impression of losing his balance in a world where everything is moving and elusive; a strange world, where one only grasps forms with vague and fugitive outlines, where things are defined, if at all, only with incredible difficulty. At other times, he will have to wrestle with the gravest problems of philosophy. And if, in the end, he were to think that Theosophy is not worth the effort which he and the author have made to grasp and judge it, our end would be attained.

Th. M.

The Principles of Theosophy

FIRST PART

THE THEOSOPHICAL DOCTRINE

CHAPTER I

STUDY OF OCCULT SCIENCE

SPIRITISM AND THEOSOPHY: DIFFERENCES AND SIMILITUDES—DIFFERENT WAYS OF APPROACHING THEOSOPHY: ITS HISTORY, ITS SOURCES, ITS CHANGES—THE INTELLECTUAL AND DOCTRINAL POINT OF VIEW—IS OCCULT SCIENCE COMPREHENSIBLE—THEOSOPHY AND THE RIGHTS OF REASON.

TOGETHER with Spiritism, Theosophy is one of the most fashionable forms of modern occultism. Between these two forms there exist unmistakable similitudes, and strong differences. In making these more precise, we shall be able to commence the study we wish to make of Theosophical principles.

* * *

Let us begin with the differences, and, in order to be clearer, let us, remark, first, that Spiritism and Theosophy have the same aim and the same ambition: to offer a real and definitive solution to the great problem of human life and human destiny.

The fundamental difference lies in the source from which Theosophy and Spiritism claim that they draw the elements of this solution, which is supposed to revolutionise our future. Whereas Spiritists speak of a *present* revelation, coming directly from the dead, from "disincarnate souls" or "spirits of space," Theosophists declare that they take their ideas from a historical tradition, as old as humanity itself, and even older than the present humanity: since the occult doctrine is supposed to have been transmitted by the children of a race now extinct, the Atlants, who had it themselves from more ancient and more mysterious beings.

In fact, it is from India and Thibet that this time-honoured science is said to have spread throughout the old world: Egypt, Chaldea, Persia, Greece, etc. On that privileged soil it found careful keepers, highly enlightened interpreters. And there it was that the founders of the THEOSOPHICAL SOCIETY, Madame Blavatsky and Colonel Olcott, went and gathered it from the lips of the Great Masters, or MAHATMAS, and of the Great Disciples, or CHELAS, and afterwards offered it to the western world, so deeply blinded by error.

Constant consultation of the dead; recourse to a millenarian tradition; such are, respectively, the characteristics of Spiritism and Theosophy. They give to each a distinct and original physiognomy.

That primary difference leads to several others, which have also to be defined.

Because he considers himself in immediate relation with the world of the dead, the Spiritist is—or at least he wants to be—first of all, an *experimentalist*, a scientist. His kingdom is that of psychical or "metapsychical" phenomena. He boasts that he can register, with a scrupulous conscience, the manifestations of the world beyond—cases of haunting, moving or talking tables, apparitions, materializations, etc. And his idea of life after death can only be and ought only to be, in his opinion, the result or the generalisation of the notions derived from the valuable help of mediums.

STUDY OF OCCULT SCIENCE

The Theosophist's method is exactly the reverse of the Spiritist's. Because he is the man of a tradition, the Theosophist receives a ready-made doctrine. For him experience is not a starting point, but a point of termination. It is not used to guide and direct research. It is used to justify, if need be, the positions adopted in bygone days by the secret doctrine. Moreover, that confirmation by facts, so much appreciated, as a rule, by philosophers, does not hold the first place in a Theosophist's preoccupations. The visible Universe is such a minute part of the " manifested " Universe, and the " subtle " worlds are so much richer than the lower planes of coarse matter where we eke out our terrestrial life, that the attention of the Theosophist is incessantly drawn towards the heights of the Invisible. And his faith in the sayings of the Masters is so complete that, even if experience did not justify his doctrine, he would not believe it to be wrong, but would suppose that the experience, or rather, the scientist, ignorant of the esoteric doctrine, is wrong.[1]

---

[1] " It is very significant that some of the greatest problems of modern science are now turning on the nature of the atom, and that scientists are asking, what is it ? Is it matter or force ? Is it a particle or a vortex ? NEVER WILL THAT QUESTION BE ANSWERED WITH CERTAINTY UNTIL MAN HAS DEVELOPED IN HIMSELF THE POWER TO RESPOND TO THE LIFE THAT THRILLS IN THE ATOM," that is, until the modern scientist has submitted himself to the Theosophical Yoga. (See Annie Besant, *The Evolution of Life and Form*, p. 21.) Moreover, it is fair to note that, nowadays, Theosophists are more preoccupied than of old in harmonizing the formula of their system with the scientific data. The time is over when one reproached Mr. A. Sinnett with having considered the highest faculties of the western world so undeveloped that he thought it proper to MATERIALIZE the doctrine, i.e. to lower on the concrete plane of physical science what ought to have been treated on the abstract metaphysical plane. It is quite clear, for instance, that Mrs. Besant "materializes" a great deal in many of her Theosophical works. There is in this a preoccupation, very explainable in itself, but which, it is to be feared, will not prove to the advantage of

In a word, a Theosophist is a speculative mind, and at the same time a believer. His first duty is to accept as a whole the ideas taught him, and his whole effort tends not towards establishing the experimental and rational value of those ideas, but towards realising, little by little, their full meaning.

How does he realise it? We shall see later on. Yet let us note now that this progress is closely linked with the birth and development of some faculties, more powerful than the common intellect of men. Provided with those faculties, the student in occultism will contemplate with a direct and intuitive vision, things, of which books give only a pale and remote description. Looking at it from the Theosophical standpoint, it might even be said that he will, when in that blissful state of clairvoyance, " experiment " the object of his faith. But let us say at once that the existence of these powers, and the means of obtaining them are, in their turn, revealed by esoteric tradition. So that, even in the one respect in which it boasts of being experimental, Theosophy is still a doctrine of authority. It makes it difficult for Theosophy to criticise religions built upon dogma. Nothing is more dogmatic, nothing is more authoritative, than Theosophical teaching.[1]

the doctrine. It would have been better for occult science to confine itself to " the abstract metaphysical plane " or, rather, to the plane of pure ideology. There is its true kingdom, and there only can it claim a serious examination.

[1] The opposed declarations, put by Mr. Leadbeater at the beginning of his *Outline of Theosophy*, cannot deceive us. To the profane, says Mr. Leadbeater (*Outline*, p. 2 seq.), Theosophy appears to be only a hypothesis to verify. And certainly, we cannot imagine it being anything else. But the verification of that hypothesis, as Mr. Sinnett affirms rather brutally (*Esoteric Buddhism*, p. 2) can be accomplished, after all, only by the development of " a great many faculties and attributes which are so utterly DORMANT in ordinary mankind that their very existence is unsuspected and the

STUDY OF OCCULT SCIENCE

Traditionalist and speculative as it is, Theosophy differs also from Spiritism by the breadth, the amplitude of its horizons. And that is easy to understand. The Spiritist, if true to his investigating methods, is bound to follow closely what he believes to be a revelation from discarnate beings. And we are taught that discarnate souls find it very difficult to enter into communication with this world. The nearest to us are the coarsest and those who know least about the after life. The farthest know best, but their astral body, made of a more subtle matter, vibrates with more difficulty in harmony with the astral body of our mediums. Thence, gaps, disharmonies, contradictions. Were we to agree to look at things from the Spiritist's point of view, we should be led to think that the knowledge of wisdom, coming from the world beyond through the dead is incomplete, fragmentary, temporary, and that, undoubtedly, many years are yet to pass before the synthesis of the "messages" can be extricated, in a clear and definitive way, from the chaos in which it struggles for the present.

Theosophy, which does not embarrass itself with the hesitations of scientific research, enters straight away into the very heart of the problems. It grasps them all, and gives to each a reply which it judges adequate and un-

---

possibility of their development denied." So that there is, PREVIOUS to the verification of the Theosophical hypothesis, an act of faith which bears on the reality of those problematic faculties, which are indispensable to the verification. In short, the student who is keen on controlling the accuracy of the doctrine has only one resource: to throw himself bravely into the water. And further, "unless the swimmer in moving them (his limbs) has a FULL BELIEF that such movement will produce the required result, THE REQUIRED RESULT IS NOT PRODUCED." (Es. Buddhism, p. 12). If that is not pure fideism, then words themselves have lost their meaning. In fact, Mr. Sinnett refuses to give a proof of the authenticity of esoteric doctrine, since "such proof cannot be given BY ANY PROCESS OF ARGUMENT."

B

answerable. Its haughty look searches heaven and earth, scrutinizes man and nature, sounds the limited and the infinite. What it teaches, concerning the destiny of the soul, and its numerous reincarnations, is only an episode in an immense action. And one must have understood the general economy of that action, if one wishes to grasp, in their real proportions, the particular and secondary events. In other words, Theosophy, the " Divine Wisdom," presents itself to us, at the first moment, as a complete system of the ultimate causes and final aims of the Universe. It includes a theodicy, a cosmology, a psychology, an ethic, even a theory of knowledge. Compared with Theosophy, Spiritism, with its stock of sporadic revelations, insufficiently co-ordinate, resembles fireflies, those luminous insects which make, here and there, bright points in the darkness of dense forests, while, above, the whole of nature is revealed in the irradiation of a mysterious moonlight.

And yet, between Spiritism and Theosophy, there are resemblances. More ; there are points of contact.

To understand clearly the nature of those relations, we must go back to the origins of the Theosophical Society. In America, before 1875, the founder, H. P. Blavatsky, had given herself enthusiastically to spiritistic practices. She was even gifted, we are told, with remarkable mediumistic powers. But—and that detail is to be underlined—Spiritism was not able to satisfy the anxious cravings of her wide awake soul. The explanations given by the dead appeared to her too simple and evidently insufficient. Not that Mme. Blavatsky thought of denying the reality of her communications with the world beyond. But she observed, in the course of her numerous experiments, disturbing quantities, problems that the Spiritic explanation was not able to solve. Then

STUDY OF OCCULT SCIENCE 19

—so we are told—she turned towards India. She became a pupil of the MAHATMAS, and learned the esoteric doctrine. She realised that the Invisible was in fact infinitely more complex than the keenest adepts in Spiritism imagine. She reached the conviction that the marvellous powers she possessed, together with other mediums, were the first thrills of a humanity destined, according to the laws of evolution, to go beyond itself. But she understood that those powers, symptoms of future progress, would be useless or dangerous, if they did not obey the principles and directions of the secret doctrine.

The initial attitude of Mme. Blavatsky has perpetuated itself in the history of Theosophy. Theosophists have always considered Spiritists as stray children of occultism, who handle forces, of the use of which they are partially ignorant.[1] Moreover, they have, on the whole of psy-

[1] In one of the last Theosophical books printed before the war *L'Evoluisme*, by Drs. A. Auvard and M. Schultz, we again find the same distrustful and doubtful attitude towards spiritists : " As to Spiritism, which under the name of modern Spiritualism, has been developed so much in some countries, we consider it a road full of perils, dangers and errors. The formation of mediums, without which spiritist séances cannot be held, is a serious anti-evoluistic action, as it disorganises the psychical unity of the being who lends himself to it. . . . The vital strength of the people present in Spiritist sittings is more or less drained by the less commendable beings of the astral plane, who try to materialise themselves ; there result serious consequences for the health and the nervous system. So a certain madness is frequent among Spiritists ; statistics show that it is a frequent cause of lunacy, which, if it goes on progressing, WILL SOON BE A RIVAL TO ALCOHOLISM. [*We* underline]. We wish to see, in the future, those objections disappear, concerning psychism as well as Spiritism, but Evoluists can but dissuade the present Humanity from using them, in the hope that humanity to come, thanks to the progress of science, will remove those obstacles, and render safe and practicable those two ways which contain powerful elements of evolution." (*Evoluisme*, p. 116).

Comforted by that thought, Spiritists, if they want to escape madness, have only to throw themselves into the arms of Theoso-

chical phenomena, and on the details of them, a very clever theory, strictly in accord with their principles.

As for the Spiritists, they have allowed themselves to be dominated by the haughty affirmations of their neighbours. Little by little, they have come to follow in the wake of Theosophy, and they borrow from it the doctrinal affabulation of their positive "experiments." In fact, there are still, in France, in Italy, in Germany, independent Spiritists who pride themselves on using the inductive methods unalloyed. And perhaps they do not look favourably on the craze of their friends for Mme. Blavatsky's or Mrs. Besant's ideas. After all, they are right, if they consider that the cause of Spiritism is seriously compromised, when it leaves the world of scientific research to put itself in tow of a preconceived system. Spiritualists have promised to give us the EXPERIMENTAL proof of survival. They wander, and they do not keep their promise, when they offer us, under the label of science, a mere succedaneum of Theosophy.

Anyhow, it will not be inopportune to remind the reader here [1] that Spiritism, as a means of more or less

phists, "responsible Masters" of the "way of occult training." (*Evoluisme*, p. 115).

[1] We are not the only ones to notice that kind of understanding between Spiritism and Theosophy. In a work on *Le Spiritisme et ses dangers* (Bordeaux, 1921), Dr. Pierre Bondou, ex-teacher at the Bordeaux Naval and Colonial School, writes as follows: "Almost all the authors who are interested in psychical research are the fourriers of Theosophy, when they are not openly its adepts, and their works can be received only with the utmost suspicion. . . There is between the two sects, a reciprocal penetration. The readers of the *Revue Spirite* adopt insensibly the Theosophical ideas, gently hinted to them in numbers of articles and books, and under that influence, the pale deism of Kardec gives way, little by little, to the neo-buddhic pantheism." (p. 180 seq.) But that is not a reason to deny to spiritists a certain "coherence of doctrine," and a certain "continuity of design." Evidently Spiritism has progressed since the time of Allan Kardec. But it has always progressed in the

STUDY OF OCCULT SCIENCE 21

noisy vulgarisation, is only a copy, and a surprisingly colourless copy, of the esoteric teaching, where the description of phenomena offers an easy opportunity for developing the themes most dear to Theosophists. Therefrom comes the resemblance that is to be observed between the two principal forms of modern occultism.

* * *

When we compared them with one another, we already suggested the method which appears to us the best for the study of Theosophy.

There are evidently different ways of studying it. For instance, we could tell its history, that is, we could tell the history of the THEOSOPHICAL SOCIETY ; we could study with suspicious attention the acts and words of its founders, and follow, through a period of about fifty years, the manifestations of its activities in the world.

Such an inquiry—as one does not doubt, since it has been made—would give interesting results. All is not clear in the origins of the famous Society. One has a right to wonder whether the faith of the first adepts in the secret doctrine was not more or less mixed with a certain amount of deception and imposture, whether the same mixture of more or less sincere credulity and of more or less clever politics has not sent Theosophists to kneel first in front of the MAHATMAS and then in front of Alcyone, whether such and such an usurpation, such and such a separation, happening at times which can be veri-

same direction. In spite of the fluctuations of thought that nobody has ever contested, there are essential points on which its adepts have never varied, and which, precisely, Theosophy enables them, to-day, to show in full light (astral double, reincarnation). And we should like to know at what time of its history Spiritism has not had the design of misrepresenting and fighting Catholicism. One must be rather blinded to shut one's eyes to that evidence.

fied by any one, have not been caused by very human feelings, insufficiently " evolved," and having nothing to do with the needs of esoteric orthodoxy. [1]

One could also make a critical examination of the sources whence Theosophists have taken the elements of that doctrine which they offer us as the very inheritance of pre-historic ages. There would be here, too, a good harvest of instructive details. One would see how Mme. Blavatsky, and her disciples after her, knew how to borrow here and there, from all religions, from all ancient philosophies, and how to build out of that enormous heap of heteroclite material a theory which does not exactly correspond to any of the documents which they had consulted. And it would not be difficult to prove that history—and pre-history still more—knew nothing of the present Theosophy up to the time of Mme. Blavatsky's enormous compilations.

Last of all, it would be possible to make sure whether, since 1875, Theosophical faith has not changed somewhat; whether some aspects of the secret doctrine have not undergone some curious transformations; whether, at the present moment, all the authors of Theosophical works or manuals have the same background of essential ideas. The work would be all the more tempting for the Great Teachers are supposed to enjoy a privilege which looks curiously like the privilege of infallibility, if it is not even stronger!

As we see, Theosophy can be investigated in several

---

[1] The reader will find plenty of articles, pamphlets, etc., on the history of the Theosophical Society, the " prodigies " done by Mme. Blavatsky, and their very natural explanations, the story of Alcyone Krishnamurti, the way in which Mme. Blavatsky confiscated, in 1883, the Eastern and Western Theosophical Society, presided over by the Duchesse de Pomar, Mrs. Annie Besant's rupture with Rudolph Steiner, and the regrettable case against Mr. Leadbeater, a present fellow-worker of Mrs. Besant.

ways. Yet, none of those we have just now mentioned will occupy us for long.

Compared with Spiritism, Theosophy appears to us a system of doctrines, a synthesis of ideas, a systematic conception of the Universe. It is only from that point of view—a capital one, evidently—that we intend to criticise and to discuss it.

It is, then, less important to know whether the founders and supporters of the Theosophical Society were sincere or not, whether or not they tried to seduce the world by reprehensible means. Persons have nothing to do with the objective account of the doctrines, and it is in no way a sin against charity to suppose good intentions at least in our adversary.

Nor shall we worry about the problem of the literary sources of modern Theosophy. Whatever its origin may be, the doctrine exists. Whether it dates from the antediluvian and pre-adamic ages, or whether it came out, all armed, from Mme. Blavatsky's brain, half a century ago it is a fact which is now under our eyes. And this fact has a value of its own, and we want to test the strength of it.

Moreover, if we wanted to demonstrate that Theosophical ideas do not agree with the originals by which they are inspired, we should run the risk of being ridiculed for forcing open doors. Theosophists have never claimed to give us, in their integral form, ideas from Egypt, or India, or elsewhere. They have never claimed to follow in the steps of Champollion, of Burnouf, of Max Müller. The worship of the letter would be, for them, equivalent to the suppression of their *raison d'être*. They take another attitude towards the sacred literature of antiquity. There is, after all, only one true doctrine in the world.

But that doctrine has taken, through ages, two distinct forms: one EXOTERIC, for the use of the masses, which are too material, too coarse, to rise higher; the other ESOTERIC, for the use of an élite consecrated by the rites of initiation. The exoteric form shows, here and there, something of the great secret which is wholly contained in the esoteric form. But the work of the Theosophist does not in the least, as one might think, consist in reconstituting, from the fragments scattered through all ancient religions and philosophies, the real and original science of the esoteric system. That system has been received by the disciples through another channel. They get it through an oral or written teaching, completely unknown to ordinary literatures,[1] and to European scientists, who look at historical sources and interpret them blindfolded. The Theosophist has first to imbue himself with that esoteric teaching. Then he comes to the exoteric documents and flatters himself that he finds in them the image of the esoteric form, weakened and often veiled by a complicated and strange symbolism. We have there a new and typical application of that dogmatic and deductive method, characteristic of modern Theosophy.[2]

[1] "The doctrine or system here disclosed in its broad outlines has been so jealously guarded hitherto, that no mere literary researches, though they might have curry-combed all India, could have brought to light any morsel of the information thus revealed." *Esoteric Buddhism*, p. 17. See ibid, p. 8.

[2] It is true that Mrs. Besant writes: "Any one who is seeking to expound the truth should be able to fortify his position from the different religions of the world, and to show that on all great, essential and fundamental truths they speak with a single voice, they teach an identical lesson." But when we come to facts, we soon find that the application of this so-called inductive method is a decoy. Let us take, for instance, the long introduction to *The Ancient Wisdom*. First, the fundamental points of occult doctrine are proclaimed. Then comes the examination of historical texts. And if it happens that the historical texts are not sufficiently in favour of

STUDY OF OCCULT SCIENCE 25

These remarks will help the reader to understand, we do not say the inanity but the insufficiency of a work which would try to ruin the authority of Theosophy by referring it to its Hindu, Egyptian or Greek sources. Even if it were proved that the works of Mme. Blavatsky, of Mr. Sinnett, of Mrs. Besant and of Mr. Leadbeater have taken much from the sacred books of India, from the Vedas, the Brahmanas, the Upanishads, the darçanas, and especially amongst the darçanas, from the Vedanta, the Samkhya and the Yoga, even if we were to establish and prove a thousand times the twists given by these same authors to the literal and obvious meaning of those ancient documents ; even if we were to be cruel enough to demonstrate—and it would be easy, although M. Maeterlinck says the contrary—that historical science has no serious proof to give of the existence of an esoteric doctrine universally known in the ancient world,[1] we should be no better off.

---

the esoteric hypothesis, remarks follow such as these : (about Mazdeism) " Reincarnation does not seem to be taught in the books which, so far, have been translated, and the belief is not current amongst modern Parsis. But we do find the idea of the Spirit in man as a spark that is to become a flame to be reunited to the Supreme Fire, and this must imply a development for which rebirth is necessary." It would be as well to say at once, that the historical documentation must comply, at all costs, with the occultist hypothesis of reincarnation. The observation can be generalized. In vain does one try to accumulate texts chosen amongst Chinese, Hindu, Persian, Kabbalistic, even Evangelistic books, the agreement of those pseudo-testimonies is only obtained with an effort, the boldness of which betrays the A PRIORI conception which directs it.

[1] Let the reader weigh carefully the meaning of these words. We do not deny that there were, in antiquity, esoteric doctrines. (See for instance, for India, *L'histoire des idées théosophiques dans l'Inde*, by Paul Oltramare, and for other countries, the monographs on the Mystery Religions, Eleusis, Phrygia, etc.). What we deny is the unity of origin and of ideas of those different esoterisms, many of which are very imperfectly known to us, if not totally unknown.

From the summits from which they claim to dominate the uncertain course of human thought, Theosophists would answer: the divergencies which exist between our ideas and the Hindu ideas, as they are known to European scientists, only prove that our doctrine is essentially neither Hindu, nor Persian, nor Chinese. It is autonomous. And if, in order to explain it, we prefer to use the sanskrit terminology, it is because India is, after all, nearer than any other country to the pure source of Theosophy; but, though near to it, yet it is no more the pure water of the source; and it is from the source that our Great Masters have drawn. As for the ignorance on the esoteric tradition, acknowledged by history, it does not impress us. How, in fact, could history know anything about it, when the said doctrine is an occult one, that is, one outside all history, and therefore, out of the reach of all scientific researches.

Extravagant though it appears, the position is worthy of argument. And it is probably thanks to that logical appearance that it is favoured by many people. "Why," say they, and M. Maeterlinck amongst them, "why should that occult tradition be, *a priori*, unacceptable and contemptible when almost everything we know about these primitive Hindu and Egyptian religions is equally built on oral tradition, the written texts being very much posterior, and when, moreover, all we are told about that tradition is curiously in accord with what we have otherwise heard."[1] It is for the esoteric tradition as it is for

---

[1] See Maurice Maeterlinck, *Le grand Secret*. That sentence of the well-known writer has the double fault of presenting the problem badly and of presuming the solution. The oral transmission does not in the least prove the primitive unity of the doctrine. As for the concordance, it has to be established by an objective interpretation of the texts, and we cannot but admire the cleverness with which Mr. Maeterlinck manages to make a stream of common ideas run through all the ancient religions.

STUDY OF OCCULT SCIENCE 27

certain suggestions which in the end settle themselves in the public mind, after having been often repeated, because, under a semblance of truth, they flatter the imagination, always in search of new and marvellous ideas.

Are there any means of solving the problem, without borrowing the endless roundabout way of the criticism of texts, which only specialists are able to follow, and which, moreover, always runs the risk of being stopped by a plea of exception from Theosophists ? That contrivance is given us by the ideologic criticism of Theosophy. The Theosophist, we agree, owes nothing to the exoteric history of religions. He resorts only to superior and mysterious authorities. Let him call them MAHATMAS or RISHIS, the actual name does not matter. Now, who are these important beings, these omniscient Masters, whose faces have never been seen, whose voices have never been heard, except by the Initiates, and perhaps not even by them. We shall see later on that they are no puppets, no beings created as though by accident, unexpectedly. On the contrary, their place is duly marked in the whole Theosophical system. They are the representative types of a greatly evolved humanity, in advance of the progress of that fifth race to which we belong, and which is now accomplishing, on our globe, one of its planetary rounds. The MAHATMAS have developed in themselves faculties and attributes which are only latent in other men. And it is owing to the development of those extraordinary faculties that they have been able to reach the " Supreme Knowledge of the Esoteric Doctrine," and to undertake the glorious duty of " Faithful KEEPERS of the SPIRITUAL SCIENCE which has been transmitted to them by their predecessors."

So the esoteric science, scornful of the profane science, exists and keeps alive in this world by an unending succession of Masters. These Masters themselves have reached such a high degree in the Universal Evolution that they are no longer subject to the law of reincarnation, although they become reincarnate in order to enlighten men.[1] In other words, the existence of these Masters is intimately related to the kind of evolutionist conception which Theosophy teaches. But if that theory is false, what will become of these precious Masters, whose superhuman attributes are, like many other things in the doctrine, a pure and simple deduction from abstract principles? It is quite possible that there may be, in India or in Thibet, people who call themselves Mahatmas. Such is not the question. The real question is to know whether the Theosophical definition of the MAHATMAS is "thinkable." It is not, if the doctrine is wrong. The rest is an equivocation and a deception. The problem of the revelation and transmission of the esoteric teaching is essentially a metaphysical problem, which only the thorough examination of the system can solve.

There remains the history of the changes which have taken place, since 1875, amongst Theosophists, in their way of understanding and teaching the doctrine. It seems that we cannot ignore this history. Is it not the best denial we can give to the pretensions of a system which claims to be "revealed" and presents itself as the perfect expression of the absolute truth? Moreover, if Theosophy exists under several different forms, it is necessary to know precisely which of those we are going to study.

Let us remark, for the last time, how useful is our method, which, instead of losing time in besieging the fortress from the outside, tries to get right inside it, and to contemplate from within the great lines of the building. First, let us take care not to exaggerate. The "changes"

[1] See *Esoteric Buddhism*, p. 4, seq.; Le Cler, *La Théosophie en 25 leçons*, p. 64, seq.

STUDY OF OCCULT SCIENCE

are not as important as could have been expected. From one end to the other of the rather short period which stretches from the beginning of the doctrine to our days, we find the same intellectual orientation, the same background of ideas, the same plan of action.[1]

But even if we believe that we might detect, amongst the different exponents of the system, graver oppositions, not only in form, but in ideas, Theosophists have in store for us an inexhaustible provision of indulgence. We must read over, with all the attention they deserve, the solemn warnings written by the author of " The Occult World " in his introduction to " Esoteric Buddhism " : " The statement I have to make must be considered

---

[1] What puzzles the profane at the beginning, is the exuberant wealth of the vocabularies. Theosophists accuse the human language of lending itself imperfectly to the translation of their vision of the Universe. It is probably for that reason that they are not particularly keen on unifying their nomenclatures and that they borrow from exotic languages an undulating and varied terminology. The drawback is serious. And, even if they had to sacrifice a little of their verbal power in order to do so, they really ought, being a hierarchically organized society, to agree once for all on the correspondence of things with the words which represent them. That little brotherly effort would greatly simplify the task of those who try to understand. With the exception of a few words, duly consecrated by use, there are not many expressions which do not admit a rather large number of readings, of strange equivalents. And that prolixity generates confusion. With a little perseverance, however, one succeeds in finding one's way and in fixing the essential notions of the doctrine, always identical.

There is a more practical explanation of that attitude. The Theosophist, persuaded that all religions have the same background of ideas, undertakes to render that identity evident to the believers of all religions. So that it is absolutely necessary for him to speak the language of his hearers. In India, Mrs. Besant uses the sanskrit terminology. In Western countries she uses Christian words. If she had to address the natives of Australia, we should probably have a new transposition of Theosophical concepts in the Arunta, or the Wiradturi language.

in its entirety before the reader will be able to comprehend why initiates in the esoteric doctrine regard the concession involved in the present disclosures of the general outlines of this doctrine as one of startling magnitude. One explanation of this feeling, however, may be readily seen to spring from the extreme sacredness that has always been attached by their ancient guardians to the inner vital truths of Nature. Hitherto this sacredness has always prescribed their absolute concealment from the profane herd. And so far as that policy of concealment—the tradition of countless ages—is now being given up, the departure which the appearance of this volume signalizes will be contemplated with surprise and regret by a great many initiated disciples. The surrender to criticism which may sometimes, perhaps, be clumsy and irreverent, of doctrines which have hitherto been regarded by such persons as too majestic in their import to be talked of at all except under circumstances of befitting solemnity, will seem to them a terrible profanation of the great mysteries. From the European point of view it would be unreasonable to expect that such a book as this can be exempt from the usual rough-and-tumble treatment of new ideas. And special convictions or commonplace bigotry may sometimes render such treatment in the present case particularly inimical. But all that, though a matter of course to European exponents of the doctrine like myself, will seem very grievous and disgusting to its earlier and more regular representatives. They will appeal sadly to the wisdom of the time-honoured rule which, in the old symbolical way, forbade the initiates from casting pearls before swine."[1]

The quotation is rather long. It is suggestive. And anyone who dares give an independent opinion on Theosophy may take it for himself. Let us resume. The

[1] *Es. Buddhism*, pp. 15-16.

STUDY OF OCCULT SCIENCE

occult doctrine is holy, sacred, intangible ; to discuss it is to profane it. It is true ; to contest it is to prove oneself ignorant and foolish.

Go and try, then, to take advantage of the small variations you think you observe in the historical development of Theosophical ideas ! They will answer you that you misunderstand. They will give you to understand that the Masters did not tell everything at first. What you believe to be a " change " is, in fact, the more explicit manifestation of an idea already presented, and presented, on purpose, in an embryonic state. The fully-open flower is different from a seed. And yet who would say that flower and seed are in opposition ? Is there not an infinitely greater difference between exoterism and esoterism on the one hand, than between the esoterism of Mme Blavatsky and that of Mrs. Besant on the other hand ? And yet Theosophists profess that esoterism and exoterism are essentially one. Consequently, it would be difficult to deny, whatever appearances be, the essential unity of esoterism itself. Such is, in our opinion, the real Theosophical point of view. And the wisest plan is to avoid those fastidious and useless controversies, where one tries to oppose old and new texts. And if, on either side, one agrees that, since 1875, Theosophical thought has become more " explicit," one will also agree to borrow the material of a loyal and objective discussion only from the most recent works, provided, of course, that they are acknowledged as orthodox by the Society.

And we shall have plenty to work upon. The enormous work of Mrs. Annie Besant—about forty books and pamphlets—satisfies all our wishes. It represents the present form of the system. The author's personality ; the important place she occupies at the head of the visible hierarchy of the Society ; the variety of the subjects she studies ; the still greater variety of the means she uses to address audiences different in the extreme, beginners as well as more advanced pupils; the constant effort to translate in a clear language, full of happy images, the most abstruse concepts; a power for synthesis which endeavours to justify the detail by the whole; finally, an undeniable warmth in which one feels an ardent desire to convince souls and win them over to the doctrine; all that justifies a preference which, however, cannot be exclusive. Even after having perused the big work of Mrs. Besant, we can still find things to glean from the works of her predecessors and fellow helpers, past or present.[1]

But this is not all. Mr. Sinnett's remarks, already quoted, raise another prejudicial question, which is sufficient to stop, on the threshold of criticism, the most daring thinkers. The Theosophical doctrine is so deep that nobody, except the Masters who possess it, can fully assimilate it.

Mrs. Besant has been good enough to soften that verdict a little. But the distinction she sees fit to introduce removes the system still further out of reach. Amongst the teachings of Theosophy, "some are," she says, "so simple and so practical that any person of average intelligence can understand and follow them, while others are so lofty, so profound, that the ablest strains his intellect to contain them and sinks exhausted in the effort."[2]

Our perplexity increases, if we realise that this inaptitude to "contain the occult science has nothing to do

[1] In a propaganda pamphlet, published by the Theosophical Society, we find the following appreciation on the *Secret Doctrine*, by Mme. Blavatsky: "I think that work must be considered as an encyclopædia or a source of documentation." Is it a delicate way of insinuating that the famous book of the founder lacks clearness and co-ordination?

[2] *Ancient Wisdom*, p. 1.

with the personal culture, more or less deep, of the student who dares try to grasp it. The cause of this inaptitude is much more serious. It lies in the inferiority of the degree of evolution reached by the élite of the present humanity, that is, the fifth sub-race of the fifth race, which includes, " the Anglo-Saxons, Germans, English, North Americans, part of the French,"[1] but part only, for the majority of the French people belong to the first sub-race, less " evolved," of that fifth race. The people belonging to the sixth and seventh sub-races would probably understand better. But the seventh sub-race has not yet appeared, and the sixth is only beginning to awake in America. Happy America, which will be for a time the very kingdom of Theosophy ! But the Americans will be wise not to pride themselves on that relative superiority, for, in order to be able fully to grasp the secret doctrine, one must belong to the superior races, escaped from humanity, freed from the inferior vehicles, living on the plane of divine ideas. To grasp it, one must be MAHATMA, RISHI, DYAN-CHOHAN, BUDDHA, names which all refer to about the same degree of specific evolution. If not, one must tread carefully and unceasingly the long and difficult path which leads to initiation. Such is one of the most important principles of Theosophy : the degree in knowledge is closely related to the degree in evolution, and to live and to know are one and the same thing.

Knowing that, we shall ask ourselves what is the use of vulgarising a teaching doomed to be misunderstood by all who are neither RISHIS nor Initiates ; especially if the new doctors undertake to enlighten the obscurity of the religious dogmas by a luminous and intelligible vision of Universe and Life ? Will not the vision be like a mirage ? We try to grasp it, it vanishes. We pursue it, it recedes,

[1] Le Cler. *Théosophie en 25 leçons*, p. 141.

always full of promises, to far away places, beyond thousands of compulsory reincarnations.

What means are left to us, who are profane, to reach it and judge it ? Thank God, reason is left.

Where religions are concerned, such as Christianity, for instance, which gives itself frankly, without reticence, as a transcendental religion, a religion with mysteries, we know where we are. Human intelligence never loses its rights, and we ask for the eternal motives which justify, in the eyes of reason, the act of faith. We make sure, furthermore, that the very object of faith is not in contradiction with the absolute laws of thought. Then we bow before the mystery, and we believe with all our hearts, with all our wills, with all our souls.

Theosophy does not allow the first of these two processes —external proofs are non-existent. They are based on the hypothesis of an occult tradition, which, by definition, escapes the control of history. Let us repeat, with Mr. Sinnett : " We may search both ancient and modern literatures in vain, however, for any systematic explanation of their [the Mahatmas'] doctrine or science."[1]

Devoid of all exterior support, Theosophy can be treated only with the second process, that is, be put face to face with the laws of logical thought. To tell the truth, Theosophy opposes to that treatment another hypothesis —a metaphysical one—according to which humanity, because of its lack of evolution, has no right to judge a doctrine which is above it. There is the very point where the conflict begins.

We consider that the laws which regulate the activity of our intelligence have an absolute value, which is permanent in all the degrees of human evolution, if there is an evolution, and still more if evolution, in the Theosophi-

[1] *Esot. Buddhism*, p. 8.

STUDY OF OCCULT SCIENCE

cal sense of the word, does not exist. What is objectively true or false, at such and such a degree of the progress, even the lowest, is objectively true or false at such and such another degree, even the highest. God himself cannot think or realise contradictory things. From the bottom to the top of the thinking hierarchy, intelligence is ruled by the supreme law of identity or contradiction.

In the name of that law, we dare to vindicate the right to express, without acrimony, but at the same time without reserve, a justified opinion on Theosophy. The " Masters " have not thought it necessary to keep their ancient secret. They have " thought it right to speak." They have foreseen, as an unavoidable conjuncture, the lack of passivity of their European hearers. They have foreseen resistance. During half a century, they have had the leisure to make themselves clear and to rectify, if necessary, the incorrect formulas used by their interpreters, speaking to a cultured and well-read public. They come back. willingly, to the common road. Through the mouths of some of their disciples, they even invite us to consider Theosophy as a pure and simple hypothesis, leaving us perfectly free either to adopt it if we find it " satisfactory," if it seems to us a doctrine which " solves more of the problems of life, answers a greater number of the questions which inevitably arise for the thinking man "[1] or to reject it, if some other system seems to us better. If that liberal invitation authorizes criticism, not only of the solutions given by Theosophists to the great problems of life, but even of those superhuman faculties which have enabled the occult science to discover the secret of the Universe, we can but accept to listen in absolute independence of mind to the teachings of the Great Masters.

That is what we are going to do in this book.

[1] Leadbeater, *Outline of Theosophy*, p. 14-15.

After giving an outline of the principles of Theosophy, we shall come back again to each of the fundamental points of the system with all the necessary details. Our only preoccupation will be to answer that primary question, on which depend all the others: Has Theosophy any right to intellectual existence? Or, in other words, can it be assimilated by human reason?

CHAPTER II

From the "One" to Vishnu

THE ONE EXISTENCE—APPARITION OF THE "CENTRE OF CONSCIOUSNESS," ISHVARA, LOGOS OR GOD—MAYA, THE KOSMIC MEMORY—LIFE, CONSCIOUSNESS AND VIBRATION—THE TRIMURTI—ORIGIN OF MATTER—THE THREE GUNAS—DEFINITION AND ROLE OF THE THREE LOGOI—THE WORK OF BRAHMA—ORGANIZATION OF THE SEVEN PLANES AND THE FORTY-NINE SUB-PLANES OF THE UNIVERSE—NAMES AND CHARACTERISTICS OF THE GREAT KOSMIC REGIONS—THE GENERAL LAWS OF EVOLUTION—THE WORK OF VISHNU—FORMS AND FORM-MONADS—THE "ELEMENTALS" THEIR FUNCTIONS AND THEIR TENDENCIES—EVOLUTION OF LIFE AND FORMS—THE DEVAS.

"WE cannot grasp our own position intellectually without some idea—however vague it may be—of our relation to the whole ; and while some students are content to work within their own sphere of duty and to leave the wider reaches of life until they are called to function in them, others feel the need of a far-reaching scheme in which they have their place, and take an intellectual delight in soaring upwards to obtain a bird's-eye view of the whole field of evolution. This need has been recognised and met by the spiritual guardians of humanity." So writes Mrs. Besant.[1] We hope not to be accused of temerity, if, putting ourselves in the class of the students who wish to have a bird's-eye view, we try to realise, as far as it can be done "at our present stage of evolution,"[2] the Theosophical synthesis. We do not know whether

[1] *Ancient Wisdom*, p. 312-313.
[2] *Ancient Wisdom*, p. 311.

the " intellectual delight " will be very great. But when it is a question of judging a doctrine, pleasure takes a second place and truth must come before everything else.

Imagine the Universe suddenly annihilated; what would remain? Go back in thought to the moment which immediately preceded the first apparition of things; what do you find? " An existence, real, eternal, infinite, incognizable "; " the One Existence "; " the inconceivable One "; " the One Being without a second "; " the Superconsciousness," situated " beyond the limits of all personality "; " the All," of whom we can only say, laconically: " He is," or, more laconically still: " THAT."[1]

" THAT," being by definition inconceivable and incognizable, the occult doctrine must needs be, concerning it, wanting in more precise notions. When it speaks of it, it contents itself with using the rather dazzling but very masterful language, which the Brahmanic tradition uses round its favourite theme: " It is not to know Him not to ignore Him completely."

And yet, the world came out of " THAT." Before we describe that process, we must first correct an inaccurate expression, which we voluntarily used. Theosophy does not admit the possibility of a sudden annihilation of the Universe, nor does it conceive the FIRST apparition of things. There is no absolute end or beginning of things. Eternally, the One Existence is at work, even when it does not work directly. But its manifestations, stretching along the immeasurable duration, are interrupted by periods of silence and rest. Those alternations of activity and of rest have been symbolised by the Brahmanic philo-

[1] All those expressions are to be found in most Theosophical books.

sophy in a striking way. Brahma—the absolute Being—breathes. If he exhales his powerful breath, the world exists, exteriorizes itself. If he draws his breath in, the world, little by little, is resorbed and disappears. Or else Brahma dreams, and the Universe is the dream of his nights. But if he falls into a deeper sleep, the dream vanishes, and nothing more exists. And as, eternally, the absolute Being breathes or sleeps, it is impossible to imagine the instant of the first kosmic manifestation, the first MANVANTARA. Each manifestation has been preceded by another manifestation, always, infinitely, going back towards the past.

From the Heart of the One Existence, a will comes forth: the desire, the will to "multiply itself." But how can the One, the Infinite, multiply itself? Is it not an insoluble contradiction? If he insists, the One Existence will have, at all costs, to consent to divide himself, to circumscribe himself, to fall from his initial perfection. And if he accepts, will he not then cease to be One and Infinite?

A middle term seems to offer itself, very unexpectedly, to conciliate these two extremes. We learn in physics that the lightening power of a focus is in the inverse ratio of its calorific power. Brought to a certain degree of heat, it ceases to be luminous. Let us suppose that through that ultra-incandescent mass we circulate colder currents; we shall see luminous patches form again at the places where these currents pass. The focus will again become partly visible.

That comparison will help us to imagine the formidable event which, in the bosom of the One Existence, precedes the apparition of the Universe. That Existence possesses, inherently, such an intensity of being, of power, of life, of consciousness, that he is at once inaccessible and incommunicable. He is, and he is not. He can, and he cannot. He is conscious and not conscious—because none of the qualities we call by these names has any common measure with him, even if we imagine a very fragile and remote relation. That radical transcendency does not allow "THAT" any immediate manifestation; he is the mass which is so hot that it seems to be no longer luminous.

But, through the Infinite Existence, a "Great Breath" has passed. Whence comes that breath? It does not come from outside, as would be the case in our example. It comes from within: It is the desire, it is the will itself of the Super Consciousness*! And the result resembles the one quoted above, when a cool current circulates through an ultra-calorific mass. Inside, on the periphery—the image does not matter here—luminous focuses light themselves: focuses of consciousness, of life, of power; we may now call them so, as they have passed from the state of absolute transcendency to a state of relative transcendency, relative to our present concepts.

So is framed, in the depths of the "One Being, without a second," what Theosophy calls esoterically "Centre of Consciousness" and, exoterically, according to the religions which have known and adored him, ISHVARA, Logos or God.[1] So does the limitless Being, without ceasing to

---

[1] We shall use indiscriminately, in the course of this book, the four above-mentioned names. Let us note that the "Centre of Consciousness" may be considered from two points of view: in its relation with "the One"; in its relation with the Universe. Its relation with "the One" cannot be better defined than by the substantial identity. For, as the lightening power virtually pre-existed before the passage of the cool current, in the igneous mass, and was identical with it, so does Ishvara virtually pre-exist in the Infinite of the "One Existence" before the passage of the Great Breath, and is identical with it. Ishvara is merged, dispersed, latent in that Existence. He is the very Existence, in so far as it is able to contract, to concentrate itself into a proper and real Consciousness. And, as after the passage of the cool current, the luminous focus goes on belonging to the igneous mass, from which it is not separated, so,

FROM THE "ONE" TO VISHNU

be himself, limit himself and become able to create a world.

For, the aim of that awakening, in the depths of the Eternal, of the Consciousness of Ishvara, of the Logos, of God, is to play the part of creator of a world. We say of A world, of A kosmos, not of THE world, of THE kosmos. " By a KOSMOS is meant a system which seems, from our standpoint, to be complete in itself . . . . Such a system is our solar system."[1]

Now, the centre of consciousness having no other *raison d'être* but to manifest itself in a KOSMOS so defined, there will be as many centres of consciousness as there are systems forming a whole, and similar to our solar system. If every one of the stars we see in the sky is a sun, there are hundreds of thousands and millions of Logoi. When, at night, the Theosophist looks up at the star-strewn vault, he contemplates, in each grain of the golden dust scattered in the sky, a focus of consciousness, springing from the abyss of the dark infinite.[2] And so we can already see the difference between the God of the Theosophical conception and the God of the Jewish, Christian or Mohameddan conceptions. Whatever may be the relation between the kosmic demiurge, Logos or Ishvara, and the incommunicable God, God represents only the divine essence as *circumscribed*, and his action does not go farther than the borders of a certain planetary system. The Theosophist has nothing to do with that One Existence, which remains, in itself, inaccessible. Nor has he anything to do with the Logoi of the other worlds. Theoretically and practically,

---

after the passage of the Great Breath, Ishvara goes on belonging to the One Existence. He is the Super-Consciousness, considered as contracted, brought back to the state of Consciousness.

[1] *Ancient Wisdom*, p. 311.

[2] "There is a numberless multitude of centres of consciousness." *Evolution of Life and Form*, p.24

he knows only the Logos of which our solar system is "the manifestation." For, as Ishvara manifests and limits the "One Being without a second," so does the planetary Universe manifest Ishvara. How does it manifest him? We must now explain.

Do not let us forget the aspect of the occult doctrine of which we were speaking a moment ago: the eternity of divine action, and the alternative character of that action. Worlds and Logoi are innumerable, but each of them is subject to the law of successive appearances and disappearances. And as, in fact, we know of no beginning to each series of alternative appearances and disappearances, a world that forms itself is never an entirely new world, but a world that appears again. Such would be an intermittent lighthouse, which has been for ever lighted at the confines of the immensity of the seas. That circumstance certainly complicates the synthetical exposé of the Theosophical doctrine. And in order to describe the genesis of a world, we wonder whether it would not be better first to tell how the world ends. We think it best to follow the first course, taking for granted some data which, logically, can only be justified in the end.

So we shall accept as a fact—it being admitted by Theosophists—that a world—ours, for instance—even when it vanishes after one or the other of its manifestations, does not disappear altogether. There remains of it a sort of memory, called MAYA, including all the forms realized during the period of exteriorization just ended.

But a memory cannot exist alone. It must have a point of connection, it must be the faculty, the attribute of a determined subject. Now, the subject of that kosmic memory is the Centre of Consciousness, Ishvara.

Why He? And, also, why is it necessary to have such a vast and such a strange memory? It is fairly easy to

FROM THE "ONE" TO VISHNU

answer this double question. As each universe is to reappear, it needs must leave of itself a vestige, an ideal model, a "pattern" according to which it will be reconstructed at the time of its next evocation. Do not let us conclude that the "pattern" will remain unchanged and identical through the innumerable resurrections of the Universe of which it is the model. The Universe evolves, progresses, during each new manifestation. And, consequently, the memory of a world that is just ending is richer in residues of experience than the memory of the same world at the end of a previous existence.[1]

As for the privilege given to Ishvara to be the subject of MAYA, it is due to the part which the great demiurge is destined to play in the work of reconstruction of the Universe.

To tell the truth, the Universe is something more than the work of Ishvara. It is an emanation of his breath, of his life. It is his life itself: "Its matter is His emanation; its forces and energies are the currents of His life; He is immanent in every atom, all-pervading, all sustaining, all-evolving; He is its source and its end, its cause and its object, its centre and its circumference; it is built on Him as its sure foundation, it breathes in Him as its encircling space; He is in everything and everything is in Him."[2] After this, any question concerning

---

[1] When studying, later on, the mechanism of reincarnation, we shall see—but on a much reduced scale—a similar phenomenon occur again. Each human being, after an ephemeral existence, keeps in himself the indelible residue of his acts, and that residue—the KARMA—is the starting point and the basis of the following existence. What KARMA is to the individual, MAYA, the kosmic memory, is to the whole of the Universe. Hence that principle of the occult doctrine: "Maya is prepared in every case by the merging in Ishvara of the whole of the Universe which is come to its ending." *Evolution*, p. 25.

[2] *Ancient Wisdom*, p. 41.

the attribution of MAYA to the Logos is useless. If the real Universe is only, after all, a manifestation of the Logos, the MAYA, which is a sort of copy of the real Universe, has the same origin.

Besides, as we have seen, the world could not exist if the Super-Consciousness did not want to contract, to limit itself. But the subjective limitation fatally brings with it the objective limitation. A subject of limited power can evidently accomplish only what is included in the area of this power. So, in other words, says Mrs. Besant : " Coming forth from the depths of the One Existence . . . . a Logos, by imposing on Himself a limit, circumscribing voluntarily the range of his own being, becomes the manifested God (that is for the subject), and tracing the limiting sphere of his activity, thus outlines the area of His Universe (that is for the object). Within that sphere the Universe is born, is evolved, and dies."[1] That limiting sphere expresses itself by MAYA, which, once more, is the attribute of the Logos.

From that analysis, let us remember chiefly that MAYA and ISHVARA are only two modalities of that Centre of Consciousness which is, at once, subject and object, and receives, in its double function, the name of SELF-CONSCIOUSNESS.

We are able now to imagine the whole of the movements which bring influence to bear on the God or Logos, maker of a Universe. During a period, the length of which is beyond all calculations, the Centre of Consciousness has remained " merged in the infinite of the Super-Consciousness." But it has not disappeared, although it was part of the pre-eminent manifestation of the One Existence. Then, one day, under the impulse of the " Great Breath," it has limited itself once more, it has inwardly concentrated itself. Around it, the memory of things was

[1] *Ancient Wisdom*, p. 41.

FROM THE "ONE" TO VISHNU 45

floating like the wreck of a disappeared world. Having recuperated that memory, it directs its attention to it. Then the powers of the SELF-CONSCIOUSNESS come into action. The world is going to be born again, manifesting God.

Let us follow attentively the progress and the stages of that resurrection.

* * *

First, let us be quite sure, once for all, of those three directing ideas which, like the signs placed at the beginning of a stave of music, give the key and the tone of the Theosophical doctrine : in the Universe ALL IS LIFE, ALL IS CONSCIOUSNESS, ALL IS VIBRATION.

Of those three ideas, the first two are evident, according to the previous explanations : " There is but one Life, the Life of God, within everything in His Universe. No Life save His Life . . . ."[1] " He . . . . (Ishvara) dwelling within, and enveloping and permeating all objects . . . ."[2] And when, presently, we shall have reached the extreme frontiers of the manifested world, when, from region to region, from plane to plane, and from sub-plane to sub-plane we shall have reached the uttermost end of the mineral world, we shall have to remember that, even there, Life and Consciousness remain. In the Theosophical system, there is a mineral life and consciousness, as there is a human life and consciousness. The difference lies only in a question of degree, that is to say, in a more or less narrow limitation of the Life and Consciousness of the Logos.

The third idea : all is vibration, expresses a theory which is special to Theosophists, although it boasts of being confirmed by recent scientific discoveries : " The Universe is made up of vibrations, the vibrations which are the modifications of the divine outpouring of life."[3]

[1] *Evolution*, p. 42. [2] *Evolution*, p. 107.
[3] *Evolution*, p. 32.

So there is equivalence between the three expressions : Life, Consciousness and Vibration.

Having admitted this, let us proceed in order, going from the general to the particular, from the principal phenomena to the lesser ones.

So far, we have considered Ishvara, Logos or God, as a single personality. In reality, this personality is threefold. It is a trinity, a TRIMURTI. And this means that it takes successively three aspects, three functions, each of which corresponds to one of the three great stages through which the Universe must go to realise the fullness of its perfection. Under his first aspect, God is MAHADEVA, Great God or First Logos ; under his second aspect, God is VISHNU or Second Logos ; under his third aspect, God is BRAHMA or third Logos. We enumerate these three Logoi, in the order of their importance : Being, Love, Mind. In fact, and, if we may say so, chronologically, they come on the stage in the inverse order.

Prior to the differentiation, Ishvara, as a whole, and without distinction of personalities, " outbreathes " primeval matter. Is this matter a real creation, something made out of nothing ? Not at all. The occult science, even when it uses the word creation, ignores, and strongly disapproves of, the sense which we attach to this word : " No one expression can have contributed more to mislead the human mind in basic speculation concerning the origin of things than the word " creation " . . . . " Our planet and ourselves are no more creations than an iceberg."[1] But if the idea of creation is to be put aside as " butting against the facts,"[2] we must suppose a pre-existing matter. Where has Ishvara, who is not a creator, been able to find the material for that Universe, of which, at the beginning, he possesses only the memory ? The question and the answer are given under that form :

[1] *Es. Buddhism*, p. 210.   [2] *Es. Buddhism*, p. 211.

FROM THE "ONE" TO VISHNU

" What existed before the manifestation of the Universe ? Nothing but the Spirit or Breath of God, and the primordial Matter or Space. Life and matter are the two opposite elements, the two poles of that omnipotence, eternally hidden, also called the Absolute, the Unmanifested. [1]

So, concerning the " Absolute," which we were told was incognizable, we know that it is able to polarise in two opposite directions : Life and Matter. Does this inner polarisation accompany the act by which the Self-Consciousness limits itself again in the depths of the One Existence, or is it prior to that act ? It does not matter much ; the real import of the text is elsewhere. We learn that Matter and Life are, in essence, identical with the " One Being, without a second." They are only derived states of that Being. And it is from that Being that *Ishvara* has drawn the material for the Universe.

So we understand why Theosophists consider they can do without creation, [1] why Mrs. Besant, writing on the same subject, does not speak of creation but of outpouring.[2] And we might be tempted to interpret the word " outpouring " according to its rigorously etymological sense, POUR OUT, send out, push forth. This interpretation seems, moreover, quite imposed on us by the way Theosophists describe the manifestation of matter in a given world : " Ishvara, the Centre of all, enveloped in Mâyâ, sends forth His breath ; as that vibrating breath falls on the enveloping Maya, Maya becomes Prakriti, or Matter—rather, perhaps, Mulaprakriti, the root of matter."[3]

[1] *Théosophie en* 25 *Lecons*, p. 21.
[2] *Ancient Wisdom*, p. 315.
[3] *Evolution*, p. 28. Is not that " vibrating breath " as a prolongation of the " Great Breath " which, as we have seen, incites the " Centre of Consciousness " to circumscribe itself once more to produce the world ? Ishvara, when he outbreathes matter, with a view to the production of a world, only canalises the impulse he has

Nevertheless, the definition of the matter outpoured into MAYA includes a reticence. The expression MULA-PRAKRITI, root of matter, must be chosen preferably to PRAKRITI. Why? Because, even after its initial production the matter is not yet fully manifested. It lacks three "fundamental, essential and invariable" qualities, the absence of which would not allow it to lend itself to the future changes it must undergo. These three qualities are the three GUNAS, so well known in Hindu philosophy: TAMAS, the inertia, the stability; RAJAS, the activity, the strength; SATTVA, the harmony. "They are present in every particle in the manifested universe, and according to their combinations is the nature of each particle.[1] The kosmic stuff, lacking consistency, would be but a weak support for the forms which must be born from it; lacking movement, it would resist the evolutive impulsion which must alter it unceasingly; lacking harmonic vibrations, it would perpetually tend towards dissociation, scattering chaos. The wisdom of ISHVARA has provided for all that: three modifications of his consciousness generate a threefold vibratory force which determines, in matter, the three attributes which have just been defined.

Henceforth, matter is apt to serve the design of God, and each of the three Logoi is going, in his turn, to begin the particular work which falls to him in the realisation of that stupendous design.

The first to enter the scenes is BRAHMA, the Mind. That priority belongs to him for reasons which will appear

received from the "One Existence," that Existence being the primeval reservoir of all the matter of which all the Kosmos will be built. And MAYA, the kosmic memory, touched by the matter-impregnated breath, begins in turn to swell with reality.

[1] *Evolution*, p. 29. It is useless to observe that the *Theosophical* conception of the "Gûnas" is not necessarily consistent with that of Hindu philosophers concerning the three fundamental properties of beings.

FROM THE "ONE" TO VISHNU

clearly when the doctrine is exposed. It will be useful, all the same, to show the way by erecting beforehand a few beacons.

Theosophy conceives of the total history of a Universe as of a gigantic evolution divided into two principal phases: a phase of involution, during which the " forms " issued from the divine life of Ishvara wrap themselves up in a veil, thicker and thicker, of kosmic matter; a phase of real evolution, during which the forms shed little by little their material wrappings, beginning with the coarsest, strengthen and exteriorize their hidden and divine potentialities, until finally they unite themselves with the one principle which is the soul of the world, that is the " centre of consciousness " mentioned before. Once more, the phase of evolution or ascension is divided into two periods. The first helps the forms to reach that degree of refinement at which they become capable of being used as the " vehicles " of the human soul. Then that soul dons the material stuff prepared by all the preceding evolution and will itself continue the ascending movement inaugurated in the lower regions of the world. Let us also note that the forms, made to journey slowly through the regions of kosmic matter, from which they borrow their constitutive elements, possess a centre, a permanent nucleus, called a monad. The human monads, living sparks of fire, sprung from the divine matter, are called, like the source from which they come, " Self-Consciousness." The infra-human monads are called only monads of form.[1]

Those rapid explanations allow us to imagine that the total development of a Universe requires a treble intervention on the part of the supreme Logos, or, to be more precise, a treble afflux of his vital strength. He must first

[1] The monad, human or not, is sometimes given the name of PURUSHA, borrowed from the SAMKHYA vocabulary. See *Evoluisme*, p. 24 and passim.

dispose the material planes of the kosmos—a sort of immense " velum " up and down which the monads must alternatively go to accomplish their involutive arc. Then, he must wrap up the monads in their forms, woven with the surrounding matter (involution) and provide for the progressive transformation of those forms (evolution). Last of all—as the human monad is not, as such, a pure product of the previous evolution—he has to " involute " the human Self " in the tabernacle it is going to occupy," and lead that " Self," gradually, to the ultimate term of its destiny.

Now, ISHVARA,[1] when he disposes the material planes of evolution, is called BRAHMA, and is the third Logos ; when he presides over the birth and evolution of the forms, he is VISHNU, and the second Logos ; when he presides over the birth and evolution of the human self he is MAHADEVA, and the first Logos.[2] So the priority of BRAHMA becomes evident. BRAHMA, to use the strong Theosophical expression, builds the " womb " of the Universe, where the vital forms infused by the other Logoi will be cast.

Let us see BRAHMA at work. In front of him lies the ocean of matter outbreathed from the Great All, and ready, thanks to the three GUNAS, to receive new and fruitful impulses. There remains but to organise this matter. Let us study attentively the process of that organisation. It gives us the key to the whole Theosophical cosmology.

As well as the other proceedings of the Supreme Logos, the activity of BRAHMA results simply from a modification of ISHVARA'S consciousness. And this means that the

[1] *Evolution*, p. 29-30.
[2] The involution of the human monad being pursued down to the lower planes of the Kosmos, it seems that, at least on those lower planes, Vishnu collaborates with Mahadeva to the evolution of man.

world, divided into separate regions, is an aspect of the kosmic consciousness. It means, moreover, that what is added to matter by the concurrence of BRAHMA is at once life and vibration.

Now, that vital vibration can be divided into seven periods, or seven successive outpourings, or TANMATRAS. The new state of matter modified by the emission of divine life is called TATTVA. To put it shortly, the TANMATRA is the vibration given; the TATTVA is the vibration received, registered by matter, or, better still, it is the matter vibrating under the action of the TANMATRA.

There are seven, as we said before, of those vibratory movements, and it is no use trying to find a rational explanation of that number. The septenary division is, in occult science, a postulate, an axiom which is not to be discussed. It is much more important for us to find the link which unites one to another those seven modifications of kosmic consciousness and matter. The secret of evolution, such as it is conceived by Theosophists, is included in the mechanism that we shall try to render intelligible.

In fact, the work is not easy. Mrs. Besant tells us so: " Try to realise this process if you can, though I know the conception is difficult."[1]

Three great laws seem to preside over the organization of the planes of the kosmos.

[1] *Evolution*, p. 31. And we are bound to say that Theosophic writers do not seem over keen on making easier, for the pupils—at least for those from outside—the access to that capital part of their teaching. The process of the formation of the planes of the world is set out by Mrs. Annie Besant, first of all briefly in *Ancient Wisdom*, ch. I, and then more explicitly in *Evolution*, ch. I and II. The majority of other Theosophical works suppose that mechanism known, and only describe its results. No doubt they fear they might, if details were given, dishearten the great public, little accustomed to that particular kind of mental gymnastics. The Initiates, who are supposed to contemplate *de visu* the structure of the Universe, have not such pains to take!

The first can be expressed as follows: the intensity of the vibratory movements or TANMATRAS is decreasing. If, for instance, we represent by the co-efficient seven the vibratory intensity of the first tanmatra, the vibratory intensity of the following tanmatras will be respectively represented by the numbers 6, 5, 4, 3, 2, 1. That law could be called, in equivalent terms, the law of the density of the material planes. The more powerful the vibration is, the more subtle the matter subject to it, and *vice versa*. And that is why, in the kosmos, the planes are superimposed according to their degree of vibratory power: the more "lively," and consequently the more subtle on top, the slower, and consequently the denser, in the lower part.

If that first law was the only one to act, the ordinance of our seven regions would be very simple. We could easily imagine it as the result of an action exercised, fan-shape, from a given centre.[1]

Now, it is not at all in that simple way that the regions of the Universe have appeared in matter, such as the seven colours of the spectrum refracted by the prism on a

[1] Imagine a circle of such vast proportions that any arc taken on the circumference offers nearly the aspect of a straight line. Join the two ends of that arc to the centre, and in the same way, divide the sector thus obtained into seven equal parts. Inscribe inside the first circle, a second one parallel to it. You will have, at the end of the operation, a strip divided into seven equal surfaces, which all converge towards the centre of the two parallel circles. Suppose now that, from that centre, seven luminous streams come forth, which fill with seven different and decreasing shades of the same colour the seven compartments of our peripheric strip: the effect of that degradation will be very harmonious. And you will probably have the impression that the most intense shade of the first compartment has spread into all the other divisions by a kind of progressive dilution. Really, such is not the case. All those compartments are and remain isolated. They do not depend on one another. Each of them only depends on the central focus which has directly produced them and placed them in juxtaposition.

FROM THE "ONE" TO VISHNU

screen. The action of BRAHMA is exercised in the very axis of the planes of the world. And that means that a TANMATRA, or vibratory wave, before it reaches the region of matter which is its aim, must cross all the upper regions, or TATTVAS, already constituted. And that second kosmic law already complicates the genesis of the kosmic planes. For it is impossible for a vibratory wave to cross a superior plane without introducing in it a modification and a kind of deterioration, since the new wave which passes is inferior in quality to the wave which it pervades. We shall soon see the effect of that mixture, for a third law intervenes, and completes the entanglement.

That third law can be translated thus: each higher plane exercises on all the lower planes an action which is particular to that higher plane, but remains in proportion with the receptive capacity of the lower planes.[1]

Such are the laws. Let us see how they work.

The first TANMATRA received in the matter determines, by the stupendous intensity of its vibrations, the highest, the most subtle, the most ethereal plane of the Universe.

The second TANMATRA passes, and, according to the second law, penetrates into the first region already constituted; it pervades that region. Thence follows a "modification" which manifests itself in a slight slackening of the vibratory movements of the first plane. But on the one hand, that slackening is not able to bring back the vibrations of the higher plane to the coefficient of the second TANMATRA, for the latter, being weaker, feels,

---

[1] An unexpected application of the well-known scholastic principle: QUIDQUID RECIPITUR AD MODUM RECIPIENTIS RECIPITUR. Is it not a proof that the laws of thought work everywhere, even in Theosophy?

in its turn, the reaction of the environment through which it runs ;—and, on the other hand, the resultant of these inter-reactions cannot affect the higher plane in its whole, as, being denser, that second tanmatra inclines downwards on its own ; and, while the upper part remains untouched, the lower part alone is the theatre of the above-described modification. So the first plane finds itself divided into two sub-regions or sub-planes. And when all the TANMATRAS will have passed, the same phenomenon of interpenetration having taken place six different times, the first plane of the kosmos will find itself divided into seven sub-planes, the first of which contains the pure element of the region, while the others contain that same fundamental element, modified, if we may say so, by the vibratory impact of the currents which have successively crossed it. Those seven sub-planes are naturally superimposed, according to their degree of intensity. But it is important to observe that all those alterations do not change at all the essence of the elements of the superior regions. If the TANMATRAS introduce a modification relative to their degree of density, they undergo, in return, the supreme action of the infinitely subtle surroundings which receive them. All the sub-planes of the first region are superior in vibratory power and in subtlety to all the lower planes and sub-planes.

If we verify to the very end the application of those two laws : density and passage, we shall note, as we can make sure by establishing a correct account, that, after the successive emission of the seven vibratory waves, the first region has seven sub-divisions, the second, six the third, five, and so on. The last region is not subdivided at all. There is an inconvenience there, as Theosophists maintain that every great region of the kosmos includes seven subdivisions or sub-planes. The reason is that there is a third law in action, the law of the

FROM THE "ONE" TO VISHNU

influence exercised by the vibratory movements of the higher planes on the vibratory movements of the lower planes.

Let us come back to our second TANMATRA. The vibratory wave enters the first region, determines there a first sub-plane, goes outside the limits of the superior region, invades the virgin matter and creates there the second region of the Universe. But this second region has hardly come into existence when the vibratory action of the higher plane begins to act upon it. And as every agent generates an effect similar to itself, the second region is modified according to the first. The vibrations of the higher part of that first region reproduce in the second a sub-region, the elements of which, because of their subtlety, occupy the corresponding place, that is, the higher part of the second region. The vibrations of the lower part of the first region do the same, and reproduce, in the lower part of the second a division also corresponding to that of the first. So, as the vibratory waves will overflow into the first region, making in it, as we have already said, seven successive and superimposed sub-planes, these seven sub-planes will act on the lower regions, as they are being constituted. And that action, coming from above, propagated, degrading itself more and more, down to the furthermost confines of the kosmic matter, will determine, in each region, the septenary division. In the end, we will have a Universe composed of seven planes and forty-nine sub-planes.[1]

---

[1] We have not yet done with that strangely complicated mechanism. A difficulty appears, but as it is only apparent, we prefer to ease the mind of the reader, to deal with it in a special note. This is the difficulty : the application of the law called the law of " passage" had already had as a result to create, inside every plane except the last, a decreasing number of sub-regions. On the other hand, the law of " causality " alone is sufficient to explain all the subdivisions

Have these explanations given a sufficiently clear idea of the process used by Brahma to build the womb of the Universe? Evidently, the subject calls for reflexion, and we agree with Mrs. Besant that that complex mechanism makes "giddy" the brain of anyone who tries to examine it closely.

However, after the emission, by BRAHMA, of the seven TANMATRAS, the Universe offers the aspect of a gigantic series of alluvial strata, the heaviest at the bottom, the lightest on top. But do not let us insist too much on that

of the last six planes. So that there is, owing to this, a redundancy. How could one phenomenon be produced twice?

The difficulty is only apparent. When the vibratory waves, overlapping one another, determine, inside the planes they cross, the first outline of subdivisions, they leave untouched the higher parts of those planes; they do not act directly upon them; they only fix their lower boundary. Pour some oil into a vase, then add some water. Owing to the laws of gravity, the water will go to the bottom and the oil will come on top, without losing anything of its purity. The water will simply have given it from below, a limit, a frontier. The comparison is quite coarse, for in the Theosophical hypothesis, all the vibratory waves, in spite of their differences in intensity, are homogeneous in nature; but it enables us, at least, to understand that the sub-planes, even outlined by the passage of the tanmatras, leave a free field and yield to a new action which prolongs the first and completes the work it has begun.

Let us take, for instance, the third tanmatra. The vibratory wave enters the first plane, determines in it a third subdivision, passes into the second plane, determines in it a third subdivision, overflows into the ambient matter and constitutes there the third region of the Universe. Now, that second subdivision of the second plane existed already, by virtue of the law of causality which worked after the passage of the second tanmatra. Therefore, the same subdivision is produced twice. And indeed, it is produced twice, but not twice in the same way. In the first case, law of causality, the action is positive and leads to a vibratory reinforcement, limited by the intensity of the agent. Between those contradictory tendencies, the balance establishes itself, and there results the definitive state of the sub-plane in question. So that there is no redundancy.

FROM THE "ONE" TO VISHNU

comparison, which is doubly inaccurate. First, a series of alluvial strata evokes immediately the idea of immobility. And such is not the case here. The successive passages of the vibratory waves let loose in matter as many storms and intense whirlpools. With them, the life of Ishvara is poured out freely, and Life has nothing in common with the dull and congealed appearance of a geological formation. Moreover, it would be misunderstanding the Theosophical thought to imagine the sub-planes of each region as strata uniformly superimposed one above the other. In reality, the septenary division leads here to the constitution of the atoms which people each region, each principal plane of the kosmos. When we speak of sub-planes, in the Theosophical sense of the word, we simply mean that the atom of a certain plane is made of seven envelopes, of seven films encased one in the other. In short, we shall be nearer the truth if we conceive the World, after the modifications which took place in the consciousness of BRAHMA, as a vast whirlpool of living atoms. The whirlpool includes seven zones, or, better, seven "concentric interpenetrating spheres, not separated from each other by distance, but by difference of constitution."[1] Each sphere, in its turn, is filled by an assemblage of innumerable atoms of a type less and less perfect. Finally, each atom is itself made of seven sheaths disposed according to their degree of density, which represent as many secondary states of the matter of the principal plane, to which they belong.

The regions of the kosmos being distributed, let us give them names, and explain their properties.

The nomenclature is rather varied. We shall adopt the most recent,[2] observing that the enumeration of the

[1] *Ancient Wisdom*, p. 57. See ibid, p. 117.
[2] *Evoluisme*, p. 25. That nomenclature is "C. W. Leadbeater's altered in a few details."

planes begins with the last one [1] to be manifested, that is, the lowest. The reason for that order is obvious. The ascending evolution having to begin on the lower plane, it is only natural to take the order in which the monads will climb, little by little, to a degree of more perfect life. According to this principle, we shall have : I. Physical plane ; II. Astral plane [2] ; III. Mental plane ; IV. Buddhic plane ; V. Nirvanic or Atmic plane ; VI. Paranirvanic plane [3] ; VII. Mahaparanirvanic plane. [4]

The names given, [5] let us pass on to the study of the special and the general properties of those different planes.

By general properties, we mean those that are revealed by the comparison between the different planes. We may, it seems, reduce them to three principal ones.

First, Life and Matter are inseparable, at all degrees

---

[1] We mean the manifestation proper to BRAHMA, for in the work of VISHNU, and still more in the work of MAHADEVA, the last plane is the highest.

[2] " Most material forms there have a brightness, a translucency, as compared to forms here, which have caused the epithet astral or starry, to be applied to them—an epithet which is, on the whole, misleading, but too firmly established by use to be changed." *Ancient Wisdom*, p. 58.

[3] That is to say, beyond (para) the nirvanic plane.

[4] That is to say, what is greatly (maha) beyond (para) the nirvanic plane.

[5] In her work, " The evolution of life and form," Mrs. Besant, addressing an audience composed mostly of Hindus, borrows straight from the Sanskrit literature a series of equivalents that we think it right to reproduce, because of the use we shall make of that book in the exposé of the Theosophical doctrine. That transcription gives the following table of comparisons :

VII	Mahaparanirvanic plane	Anupadaka.
VI	Paranirvanic plane	A'kasha
V	Nirvanic plane	A'dilattva.
IV	Buddhic plane	Vayu.
III	Mental plane	Agni.
II	Astral plane	Apas.
I	Physical plane	Prithivi.

and on all planes. That is to say, there is no state in which Life could exist independently from the material subject which it impregnates. That law is absolute, and suffers no exception. It was already proved by the fact that the primeval matter is exteriorised by Ishvara's vital breath. But it is, first of all, the strict consequence of the principle by virtue of which all the TANMATRAS are received in a pre-existing matter. Not only there exists no matter without life, but there is no life without matter either. That inseparability of the two fundamental elements of the Universe deserves our particular attention. Theosophists will often use the words " soul " or " mind." A badly informed reader could suppose that the occult doctrine professes the existence of what is called, in the language of Christian theology, "separate soul," " pure spirit." It does nothing of the kind. The only name that can apply exactly to the meanest atoms as well as to the highest ones in the Universe is the name of spirit-matter. Mrs. Besant uses it in " The Ancient Wisdom," and the following extract will show what she means by it : " The word ' spirit-matter ' is used designedly. It implies the fact that there is no such thing as ' dead ' matter ; all matter is living, the tiniest particles are lives. Science speaks truly in affirming ' No force without matter, no matter without force.' They are wedded together by an indissoluble marriage throughout the ages of the life of a Universe, and none can wrench them apart. Matter is form, and there is no form which does not express a life ... Even the LOGOS, the supreme Lord, has during manifestation, the Universe as His form, and so down to the atom."[1] Let us remark, by the way, that, according to that text, the manifested God, Logos or Ishvara, is not a pure spirit.

Secondly, from the top to the bottom of the hierarchy of the planes, the only difference to note between the

[1] *Ancient Wisdom*, p. 43-44.

atoms of each region is the one resulting from a more or less intense vibratory state, and from a more or less refined subtlety. That law is but a corollary of the definition of matter given by Theosophists: " All matter is in essence the same. Astral matter does not differ in its nature from physical matter any more than ice differs in its nature from steam. It is simply the same thing in a different condition."[1] The scale of these progressive states of vibration and of subtlety is based on the reach of man's physical senses. The classical comparison is given by the example of the ultra-red rays. Those rays escape our sight, owing to the prodigious development of their vibratory power. So, " each state of matter on each plane .... corresponds to a vibratory state, always greater and greater and, if our senses were subtle enough to perceive them, we should see that there are, on each plane, between each degree, differences as important as those that exist between the three states known to us: solid, liquid and gaseous. This will enable us to perceive the infinite variety of aspects taken by matter in nature, and, at the same time, the extreme degree of subtlety it reaches, as we go higher through the planes."[2] We shall readily admit that infinite variety of aspects, if it is true that beyond the three degrees or states of matter known to us—solid, liquid and gaseous, there are forty-six others, more and more fluid, more and more ethereal. What can be the aspect of the forty-ninth state of matter, at the top of the mahaparanirvanic plane !

Thirdly, and lastly, the structure of the atom of a lower plane reflects the structure of the atom of the superior planes. That law is the consequence of the causality exercised by the superior level on the lower ones.[3] There is only reflection, or, if you prefer, likeness, because, as

[1] C. W. Leadbeater, *Outline of Theosophy*, p. 26-27.
[2] AGENS AGIT SIMPLE SIBI.   [3] *Evoluisme*, p. 26-27.

they came down from one plane to another, the vital emanations lost more and more of their primeval subtlety and vibratory intensity.[1]

That kind of omnipresence of the life of the higher planes of the kosmos in the lower planes occupies, in the Theosophical doctrine, an absolutely capital place. It legitimates the principle so often invoked by the champions of the system ; the principle of the absolute continuity of the regions of the Universe, and the possibility, for an atom situated on the lowest degree of the hierarchy of beings, to reach the highest degrees. If, indeed, the physical atom contains in its depths the matter and the life of the superior atoms, why, by letting free these latent potentialities, could it not become, slowly, equal to the perfection of those atoms, which are infinitely beyond it ?
" As," says Mrs. Besant, " oxygen can be reduced from the gaseous condition to the liquid and the solid, so it may be raised from the gaseous through four etheric stages, the

[1] Let us take as an example the physical atom of the first plane or Prithivi : " All that is physical is made up from the PRITHIVI TATTVA. Not only is this so, but within the limits of this physical region, correspondences of all the higher six atomic forms are reproduced. The sub-divisions of the physical region, due to combinations of the Prithivî Tattva, show forth the characteristics of the great regions which make up the Universe ; so that we have here in our solid, liquid, gas, three ethers and atoms, correspondences of the six higher tattvas, but we have them all in their Prithivî form ; they are the modifications of Prithivî, reproducing on a lower plane the great primary element." (*Evolution*, p. 34). The same idea reappears elsewhere in a form no less categorical : " On the physical plane, the physical atom is a mass of five interpenetrating spheres, in which is present as life the whole of the matter and the life of the worlds above it, the envelope, or wall, of the physical atom alone showing forth any characteristics of the physical world." (*Evolution*, p. 34). Mrs. Besant speaks here of five spheres. In reality, there are seven ; but we shall see later on that the two central spheres corresponding to the paranirvanic and mahaparanirvanic planes are as good as unknown, and practically one never takes them into account.

last of which consists of the ultimate physical atom, the disintegration of the atom taking the matter out of the physical plane altogether, and into the next plane above."[1] And Mr. Leadbeater writes, for his part: "Physical matter may become astral, or astral may become mental, if only it be sufficiently subdivided, and caused to vibrate with the proper degree of rapidity."[2] The only obstacle to that travelling of the atom through the planes of the Universe is precisely the denser envelopes which paralyse the vibratory movement of the subtler envelopes; but, if that obstacle were to disappear, if those envelopes or outer shells were to melt, the atom, transformed, would ascend—but much more slowly—as the bubble comes up from the bottom to the surface of a recipient.

Such are the general properties of the matter of the kosmic planes. They are logically deduced from the mode of activity of Brahma. They take us straight to the very heart of the Theosophical system, and enable us to reduce the occultist conception of Evolution to its more comprehensive and more universal formula. That formula can be condensed in the three following articles:

The possibilities of an atom situated on an inferior plane are limitless; anything can become all.

The evolution of the atom on a given plane is accomplished owing to the successive coatings, which constitute the atom, beginning to vibrate, the densest vibrating first.

The passage of the atom from a certain plane to a higher one takes place when the most subtle envelope of that atom, freed from its external envelopes, vibrates in unison with the densest atomistic envelope of the immediately superior plane.

The same formula can be expressed more concisely still:

[1] *Ancient Wisdom*, p. 46.
[2] *Outline of Theosophy*, p. 38.

FROM THE "ONE" TO VISHNU

" In fact, evolution may be summed up in a phrase : It is latent potentialities becoming active powers."[1] We have no hesitation in proposing, even now, that general view of the Theosophical Evolution, for, really, it is then, at the instant, that is, when the regions of the kosmos are outbreathed with the vibrating breath of ISHVARA-BRAHMA, that we must fix the frame of the universal making of things. In those few principles, apparently so abstract, all the rest of the Theosophical teaching is contained as a germ and a promise. And anything it does not include can justly be treated as a redundancy or as a datum in contradiction with the essential structure of the system.

We have now to describe, rapidly, the special properties of each plane. Rapidly, for a description of that kind will be instructive only after the setting in motion of the energies of VISHNU, the second Logos. Do not forget that this is only the first act of the great kosmic drama, the protagonist of which is BRAHMA. Now the part of the third Logos, as we have seen, is only to prepare the matter of the Universe. So, it is out of question, for the present, to inventory the formal contents of the different regions of the Kosmos, but only the aptitudes which each of them will bring to the service of the second Logos. A word will be enough to characterise those aptitudes, relative to the degree of subtlety and vibratory power of the surroundings to which they belong.

In that sense, the physical plane is characterised by the aptitude to enter into the composition of physical forms, solid, liquid, gaseous, and, beyond, etheric. The astral plane is characterised by the aptitude to produce passion-forms, sensations, emotions. The mental plane is characterised by the aptitude to produce thought-forms. The

[1] *Ancient Wisdom*, p. 44.

buddhic plane is characterised by the aptitude to form the "bliss-body" which is, for man, the fruit of pure love. The nirvanic plane is characterised by the aptitude to register the archetypes of all the inferior worlds, and to realise the conditions of pure existence for the human beings who reach it. No definition is given of the two superior planes, paranirvanic and mahaparanirvanic: "Those are far beyond our knowing, we cannot think so far."[1]

Evidently, that very dry enumeration does not satisfy our curiosity. It has at least the advantage of showing the marvellous effects that can be produced by the progressive reinforcement of a vibratory wave. Solids, liquids, gases, ether, emotions, thoughts, pure love, archetypal ideas—all that is only diversely dosed vibration. All that, moreover, represents modifications which took place in the consciousness of ISHVARA, acting as BRAHMA.

* * *

But the work of Brahma is done. The time for action has come for VISHNU,[2] second aspect of Ishvara, and second Logos of the TRIMURTI. In a few words, the author of "The Ancient Wisdom" characterises the part played by this Logos: "When the evolution of materials had reached a sufficiently advanced state, the second great life-wave from the Logos gave the impulse to the evolution of form, and He became the organising force of His Universe, countless hosts of entities, entitled Builders, taking part in the building up of forms out of combinations of spirit-matter. The life of the Logos abiding in each form is its central controlling and directing energy."[3] That text contains the assertion of four new principles.:

[1] *Evolution*, p. 33.
[2] Also called A'nanda. See *Evolution*, p. 19.
[3] *Ancient Wisdom*, p. 48.

FROM THE "ONE" TO VISHNU 65

(a) As VISHNU, Ishvara organizes forms;
(b) His life resides in the heart of each of them;
(c) He causes them to evolve;
(d) He is helped in the accomplishment of his work by entities called "builders."

Let us give a rapid commentary on each of those affirmations.

Generally speaking, forms are constituted by the agglomerations of the atoms of spirit-matter, taken from the different planes, round an inner centre, which, as we have said, is called "monad of form," as opposed to the "human monad," about which we shall hear later on.[1] But it is important to discern carefully the two stages which the monad will have to go through in order to accomplish its total cycle: a stage of coming down or involution (descending arc); a stage of ascension or evolution (ascending arc).[2]

Let us first see the action of VISHNU on the descending arc. His manner of action reminds us of that of BRAHMA. The second great vital effusion is outpoured from plane to plane, as far as the ultimate limits of the physical plane. But the effect realized here is more varied, and, chiefly, more complex.

The ignorance acknowledged by Theosophists concerning the happenings on the two superior planes—VII.

---

[1] Chapter III.

[2] To avoid confusion, let us note that the involutive stage, as preparatory to the evolutive one, is included in the general outlines of evolution. So that there are, in Theosophy, two senses of the word evolution: a broad sense, including at the same time the involutive and the evolutive stage; a strict sense, only to be applied to the second stage, the stage of properly called evolution. For the use of the broad sense, see for instance, *Esoteric Buddhism*, p. 137, and *Ancient Wisdom*, p. 186. In the following pages, we shall use the word in its strict sense.

E

and VI.—dispenses us, of course, from attempting the least description of the forms appearing in those high and inaccessible regions. In fact, we only begin to be able to stammer something when the life of VISHNU begins to overflow into the fifth plane, nirvanic or A'KASHA. But, there, we witness a phenomenon of considerable importance for the future destinies of the Universe, for A'KASHA is the place where are manifested all the antetypes and the archetypes of all the forms which are, in the future, to spring forth on all the inferior planes. One could object that those archetypal forms [1] exist already in the MAYA or memory of the vanished world. The difficulty is easy to solve. In MAYA, the forms pre-exist, no doubt. But they are not manifested, not exteriorized. They become such when they have been received in the appropriate "womb," that is to say, in the fifth plane. Moreover, it is very difficult to imagine exactly the state of the archetypal forms. They are not concrete and individualised objects. Nor are they pure abstractions, for they are at once real and active. We are asked to consider them as the synthesis of the properties common to all individuals of the same class. Let us pass on, however. The divine life of Vishnu generates first some "types" or "archetypes." Then, "by the sub-division and multiplication of those, the whole universe of concrete objects is formed; each one of them is capable of generating innumerable forms that reproduce its own characteristics amid endless diversities of subsidiary properties."[2]

That work of dividing and multiplying is made easier by the collaboration of some helpers, the notion and part of which are one of the most obscure, of the strangest points of the occult doctrine. Those helpers are the

[1] About the word "form" used in respect of the worlds which are "arûpa," that is to say, formless, see farther on.
[2] *Evolution*, p. 104.

FROM THE "ONE" TO VISHNU

"Elementals." Theosophists, it appears, have excellent reasons not to divulge the secret which wraps up the nature and operations of those singular entities. We do not in the least boast of elucidating that secret. If we compare the rare and oblique texts in which an allusion is made to it, here is what we can perceive.

Evolution, as we have already said, is "latent potentialities becoming active powers." And the centre, the subject of those potentialities, and of those powers, is the monad. But, by itself, the monad possesses neither of them. It possesses them only in its form. To be more accurate, the monad is life, a life which can be manifested, can exteriorise itself, only with the help of form. So, before developing its formal powers, the monad must wrap itself up in the corresponding formal potentialities. And that is why the involutive phase comes before the evolutive one. In that sense, Mrs. Besant writes very justly: "Coming downwards, Ishvara imparts qualities and attributes."[1] The monad would never be able to reach the different degrees of perfection which are reserved for it, if it had not been previously qualified by all the potentialities which it will have to evolve into powers, that is to say, into acts. And as, in the Theosophical conception, it will have to come up to the mental plane,[2] it needs must, during its descent, contract affinities with the three lower planes of the Universe, mental, astral, physical, the latter marking the turning point of the evolutive curve.

Now, this collation of potentialities raises a serious problem. Imagine a monad, issued from Vishnu's life. The term of its future evolution being the mental plane,[3] it must be, during the descent, deposited, so to speak, on that plane. There it attracts a certain number of atoms:

[1] *Evolution*, p. 133.   [2] See Chapter III.
[3] Below the plane of the archetypes.

the affinity is contracted. But here lies the difficulty. If, by means of attracting the atoms of the mental plane, the monad were to acquire a definitive stability, it would stop in its descent, and the evolution, the real starting point of which is the basis of the physical plane (solid state of matter) would be no longer possible. A double condition must be fulfilled, in order to solve the problem. On the one hand, the monad must stay on the mental plane long enough to acquire the necessary affinities with that plane ; on the other hand, the same monad, charged with mental magnetism, or, if we may say so, " mentalised," must go on its way, and be as if pushed from below, up to the astral plane, where it will have to acquire new affinities, in harmony with that plane. And here the difficulty appears again. If the monad were to acquire in the astral region a definitive stability, it could not reach the physical region, and the ulterior evolution could not take place. So that it must be at the same time laden with astral potentialities, and dragged still lower, through the strata of the physical planes. There, the inconvenience disappears. There are no more regions below the physical plane, to which the monad could have to descend. And nothing is opposed to its acquiring a state of formal stability, from which the ascending evolution will begin.

Now, it is easy to understand—if, of course, we adopt the Theosophical point of view—that that sort of activity which consists alternatively in holding back and pushing away the monad, in weighing for it the quantity of matter which it needs in order to acquire the mental or astral potentialities, but without being prejudicial to the exigencies of the general laws of evolution, requires a sort of discernment, of intelligence, a rather acute sense of adaptation, of harmony. The monad is not yet ready to use that discernment, as, although capable of becoming all, it is nothing as yet, since it lacks form. Therefore, the intelligence, the sense of adaptation are the properties of the atoms of spirit-matter which have a sort of presentiment, of instinct of the kosmic laws. In as far as they are called to fulfil the double part that has just been described, they are called ELEMENTALS, and their manifold combinations constitute the ELEMENTAL ESSENCE.

And so we are face to face with that paradoxical conception, which, let us frankly acknowledge it, bewilders our habits of thought ; the primordial elements constituting the forms which are being stabilised, are living entities, and their life is distinct from the life of the monad. Properly speaking, they are no longer cells participating in the one and simple vitality of the animating substance which informs them : they are sorts of hypostases, conscious or half-conscious, which aggregate and cling to each other to build the first lineaments of the form itself. On principle, there ought to be only two categories of those, one belonging to the mental plane, the other to the astral plane. But, as we shall see later on, the mental plane is subdivided in its turn into two principal regions, properly called MENTAL and CAUSAL, so that Theosophy distinguishes three classes of hierarchised elementals, always according to their degree of subtlety. To each of these it gives the importance of a real kingdom in nature, and that is why, finally, the secret doctrine distinguishes seven kingdoms : three situated on the descending arc, these are the three ELEMENTAL kingdoms ; one situated at the turning point of the descending arc, that is the mineral kingdom ; three situated on the ascending arc, these are the vegetable, the animal and the human kingdoms.

As to the strange vital property that esoterism attributes to the elementals, it has, if we just consider it for one moment, nothing to astonish a Theosophist. It is only one of the numerous applications, perhaps unexpected, but logical, of that first principle which we were underlining at the very beginning of this work : in the Universal all is consciousness. The least atom is a reflection of the universal consciousness.

Before leaving the elementals, let us point out another of their attributes. Because, owing to the part they play, the elementals are orientated in the sense of the descending arc, they have, and always keep, the same tendency to drag the monad to the lower regions of the kosmos. Now, when the monad ascends again, little by little, through the planes through which it first descended, it will have, once more, to cross the elemental kingdoms. No doubt, at that time, its form will have gained a greater consistency, according to the laws of evolution. Nevertheless, it will run the risk of being dragged downwards, or at least hindered in its ascent, by those whirlpools of elementals which will besiege it as clouds of buzzing insects. Let us transpose in concrete language these terms which are too vague or not expressive enough. On the astral plane, elementals are emotions, passions, sensations ; on the mental plane, elementals are thought-forms. While the monad tries to climb upwards, the contrary stream of emotions and thoughts will weigh upon it from above. And it will have to go painfully up the stream ; and this struggle is all the more unavoidable as it is, in fact, in that elemental environment that the monad will find the materials for its progressive growth. According to the inferior or superior quality of the sensations or thoughts it will have assimilated, it will go upwards or remain stationary. And we have already there a remote glimpse of the drama which gives Theosophy the strange attraction it has for some souls ; the drama of successive lives, with its four acts, linked together and rhythmical; existence, purification in KAMA-LOKA, co-ordination of experiences in DEVACHAN, and, finally, reincarnation.

But we have not yet reached that point of the doctrine. Let us end the description of the descending curve : " As that life-wave descends into denser and denser matter, it draws together more and more separate forms, that become denser in their nature, until at last, through kingdom after kingdom,[1] it comes down to the mineral forms, where life is most restricted in its operations, where consciousness is most limited in its scope. This is the process of the involution of life in matter, the descending arc. From this lowest point the life ascends, revealing more and more of its powers, and ordinary western " evolution " begins here, the earlier process being ignored."[2]

And, truly, the western science ignores that " earlier process." It deposits, at the origin of things, a more or less shapeless matter, moved by more or less diffuse forces. And it clashes against an insuperable inconvenience : how can " the more " come out of " the less " ? Occult science boasts of escaping this contradiction. Before evolving, matter and life have been " involuted." The links of the hierarchy of forms are joined together with absolute continuity from the bottom to the top and from the top to the bottom. The humblest mineral contains infinite potentialities. And chiefly, through the immense series, circulates the one and omnipotent impulse of the life of ISHVARA. Is not the ball which rolls down a slope gathering in a potential force which will enable it to go up the opposite slope ? Well, that is similar to what happens in the Universe, as conceived by Theosophy. The moulding of the forms is not the work of an amorphous energy, climbing, we do not know by

[1] Evidently, the three elemental kingdoms are meant here.
[2] *Evolution*, p. 106.

what miracle, from naught to the infinite. It is the work of an energy, restrained, it is true, but determined to reach its end, and energy which is only, after all, like matter itself, a modification of the consciousness of Ishvara, acting as VISHNU. We were told, a moment ago, that VISHNU resided in all forms. It is not enough to say so: "ISHVARA dwells within, envelops and permeates everything." Not only does he dwell within the form, of which he is the real centre; he is outside, too. He constitutes the environment in which the form moves, develops, increases, in which, in short, it evolves. The plant draws from the earth nourishing substances, it grows according to the potentialities of its nature; it borrows light and heat from the atmosphere. So it is with the forms emanated from the life of VISHNU. But, here, everything is divine, everything is a manifestation of the Supreme Life. Here, the soil is the spirit-matter, and the spirit-matter is Brahma manifested. Here, the nature of the plant is its form, and its form is VISHNU manifested. Here, finally, the atmosphere is again, and ever, the divine life, which, little by little, with infinite "patience" will solicit the subtlest "envelopes" of the atom to release their potentialities, paralysed by the coarser envelopes.

For, as we have guessed, the evolution of forms is only the evolution of the atoms of which they are made. But what, in the past, when Brahma alone was at work, was only a promise, as the mould is the promise of the golden coin it will shape later on; what, on the descending arc, was only an outline of VISHNU, as the child is an outline of the grown-up man, will become a progressive, a more and more perfect reality.

And how will that evolution, which will require an immeasurable time to be completed, unfold itself?

Let us consider at once the first plane, the physical

plane. At the base of this plane, at the ultimate degree where the involutive arc turns and becomes the evolutive one, stands the coarser of all beings, the mineral, the solid. But do not let us be deceived by appearances. As it was going down, like a diving-bell being immersed in the depths of the ocean, the monad was collecting booty and was attaching to itself those combinations of elemental essences, which gave it a temporary form, an outline of its future form. Or, if you prefer to say so, the monad surrounded itself with halos borrowed successively from the matter of the mental plane and of the astral plane. So that, at the extreme base of the physical plane, the solid envelope of the mineral hides a multitude of potentialities, richer and richer, vaster and vaster. The solid is liquid in latency, and, under that aspect, is no longer visible ; the ether is in latency to be transformed into three other etheric states, the last of which is in latency to be assimilated by the astral plane. On the astral plane, the same encasing exists again, and each of the seven shells of sub-planes is in latency to be assimilated by the shell which is immediately superior to it, so that the last is in latency to be assimilated by the mental plane. This is what the Theosophist's eye can discern under the rigid coating of the humblest stone on our roads.

But there is a drawback. Those encased potentialities paralyse each other. Or, to be more accurate, the external envelope paralyses, because of its density, the more fluid envelope which it contains : the solid state paralyses the impetus of the liquid potentiality ; the latter paralyses the impetus of the gaseous potentiality, and so on, to the end of the series. And then the whole problem of evolution consists in grasping the secret by virtue of which the inner vitality escapes the bondage of the external envelope and frees itself from it as the butterfly frees itself from the chrysalis. But here, there is not only one chrysalis, there are ten, and more. And we must imagine that at each step of the evolution, from the remains of a dead butterfly, another butterfly frees itself, more and more brilliant, more and more beautiful.

The release of those potentialities is done through a vibratory interaction exercised in a double way: from the outside, by the atomic environment; from the inside, by the impulse of involuted life. But, in both cases, it is Vishnu who gives the impetus to those mutual reactions. Living inside the form, since the formal monad is a spark of his life, he incites the involuted powers to answer the external vibrations. Living outside, he gives to the atmosphere of atoms a vibratory movement which solicits the sleeping potentialities to re-act. The effect of those ceaseless exchanges is to fortify little by little, the envelope underlying the peripheric one. Strengthened, that envelope frees itself, and acquires the dignity of a "vehicle." Hence comes that other Theosophical axiom: on the ascending arc Ishvara-Vishnu "builds the qualities and attributes into vehicles."[1]

How does that mechanism, the implacable precision of which does not leave anything to chance, translate itself concretely? Let us ask Mrs. Besant to explain it. Nobody has described in more appropriate and more striking words the stupendous spectacle of the kosmic evolution, as it appears to the eyes of the Theosophist, during the first stages of the Universe:

"The life within the stone has the capacity to respond, but in a very limited fashion, partly owing to its germinal nature, partly owing to the rigidity of its surrounding vehicle; therefore the brooding life of Vishnu, nourishing this germ, at once stimulates it by impacts from without and gradually modifies the rigidity so as to make progress possible. Long, long remains the life embedded in this

[1] *Evolution*, p. 133.

rigid material, working from within outwards, as all life works, playing upon and thus softening the rigidity, and slowly giving the form more plasticity in response ; we can sum up the whole of the working of the life, as the receiving of vibrations from matter without and the answering of vibrations from itself within. Notice in the earliest stages how tremendous are the impacts ; if you go back to the time when the world knew no humanity, how gigantic are the operations of nature showing herself in the mineral forms ; earthquakes, eruptions, crushing and grinding of materials, disintegration and reconstruction, all on the mightiest and most gigantic scale ; under all that, the life, trying to make the matter more plastic and able to answer more readily .... We see the life within the stone beginning to vibrate more actively as the tremendous blows come upon it from without ; and mass is thrown against mass, and mountain is piled upon mountain, until at last those mineral materials gain larger power of transmitting impulses to the life within ; the impulse coming through more strongly because of the lessened opposition from the form, then life responds more actively and begins to evolve, developing more definitely the power of response ; as this process is repeated over and over again, the life within the minerals vibrates with ever increasing rapidity, and the matter yields to it with ever greater readiness, until a stage of plasticity is reached at which the beginnings of the vegetable world can be brought into existence. Between mineral and plant in the lowest stages no definite dividing line can be drawn by science. So general is the absence of dividing lines in nature that a separate kingdom has been recognised as including low types of both vegetable and animal, and between the vegetable and mineral kingdoms a class is recognised in which the rigid crystal which belongs to the mineral kingdom has become the plastic crystalloid that belongs to the vegetable,[1] maintaining the outline of the mineral form, but showing the plasticity of the vegetable and thus yielding far more readily to the moulding influences of the life within. The life thus encased in more plastic material receives vibrations from without more easily and responds more strongly, until in the ascent that it is beginning to make, it adds the early beginning of a power of consciousness that in the mineral was not present. We call it sensation : the power of feeling pleasure and pain, the power of responding to the outside impact by a feeling within the life. After the life in the mineral has developed the power of response, the next stage in evolution is that the response takes on the sensation of pleasure and pain, appearing as that within the life which responds severally to harmonious or discordant impact from without. As the life develops this power of sensation, progress becomes more rapid. The animal kingdom is gradually builded and the power of sensation is the great characteristic which is developed through that kingdom, until—the animal forms having been rendered plastic through many ages by the impulse of life, and the life having formed and strengthened the power of responding by pleasure and pain to harmonious or discordant vibrations—the next stage is ready to be taken, the building of the vehicle for man."[2]

Such is the succession of the progressive manifestations of life. The law that presides over it involves a consequence, perhaps secondary, but worth noting. In the Theosophical system " always the organ comes after the function."[3] For the potentiality, according to the principle of evolution, being always anterior to the development of the vehicle, " through the organ the function

---

[1] Needless to say, we leave to Mrs. Besant the responsibility of this interpretation of the habits of crystals and crystalloids.
[2] *Evolution* 106-109.   [3] *Evolution*, p. 155.

FROM THE "ONE" TO VISHNU 77

expresses itself more and more perfectly."[1] The evidence of this reasoning appears more clearly if we replace the words potentiality and vehicle by the words function and organ. So, in man " the brain .... has been formed under the vibrations of intelligence,"[2] and they make a crude mistake, who say that thought is a physical secretion of the grey matter.

Let us add, to make it clear to the reader, that the evolution of the mineral accomplishes itself entirely on the physical plane; the evolution of the vegetable, started on the physical plane, goes on and ends on the astral plane; the evolution of the animal, begun and largely developed on the astral plane, becomes complete in the inferior regions of the mental plane.[3]

We cannot, at present, follow the ascending movement of life further. In the higher part of the mental plane begins a new cycle, characterised by the apparition of the human monad. Over that cycle presides another aspect of God. Let us, nevertheless, keep in mind the sketch already made. After the birth of man, it will not be modified in its essence, even on the highest planes of the kosmos: synchronical exchanges of external or internal vibrations, leading to the formation of vehicles expressing perfectly the deep potentialities of involuted life. In the meantime, Vishnu is really the master of the destinies of the kosmos. But he does not act alone. He is the lord of an innumerable multitude of entities which co-operate with him. The planes of the Universe are inhabited by " vast hierarchies of beings .... ranging from the lofty Intelligences of the spiritual regions to the lowest sub-conscious Elementals of the physical world."[4] We know the Elementals—strange entities which are at once builders and materials, of the forms in the making.

[1] *Evolution*, p. 155.
[2] *Evolution*, p. 155.
[3] *Evoluisme*, p. 27.
[4] A. Besant, *Karma*, p. 10.

It is the moving mob of anonymous workers. It is the dizzying swarm, similar to those milliards of animalculæ which gradually build up the coral rocks.

As to lofty Intelligences, we shall see later on where they come from, for their existence is linked to the unfolding of the drama of reincarnation. So, their part can be defined briefly: it is to " guide evolution according to the design of Ishvara."[1] And then, the study of this subject would not add anything essential to our knowledge of Theosophical principles. We could even omit it, if those DEVAS or Gods had not the advantage of helping us better to define the attitude of Theosophists towards all religions. When we deal with this last problem, the DEVAS will become interesting for us. Then only shall we find them again.

But the second episode of the kosmic history is ended. The third announces itself with the coming of MAHADEVA, third LOGOS, third manifestation of ISHVARA. And that third episode also requires to be followed very closely, for, if, from the theoretical point of view, it is less important than the other two, practically, it attracts us more, since it carries our attention back to the Theosophical ideas which to-day have fallen into the domain of vulgarisation.

[1] *Evolution*, p. 54.

CHAPTER III

MAHADEVA

Man is not an evolved animal—the human monad, work of mahadeva—fusion of the monad of form and the human monad—pre-existence of the "souls"—fundamental character of the human monad—"self-consciousness—rupa and arupa worlds—involution of the soul—the three stages of human evolution—development of the mind—"individuality" and "personality"—the four stages of the evolution of the "thinker"—man and his "bodies"—the mechanism of reincarnation—the development of "love"—the development of "pure" existence—planetary rounds and human races—the end of a world.

" A stone becomes a plant, the plant an animal, the animal a man, the man a spirit, and the spirit a God."[1] That occult saying fails because it is too concise. It allows us to suppose that the Theosophist, servile disciple of Darwin, proclaims that man descends directly from the animal. The supposition is gratuitous and unfair: "The true theory of evolution is different from the somewhat crude view that there is a regular succession of beings from the animal to the man. The matter has been made plastic in the animal, but man in his form is the result of a higher working."[2] That higher working is connected with a "third outpouring of divine life," which proceeds " neither from the Third (Brahma) nor from the Second (Vishnu), but from the First Logos, therefore called

[1] *Evoluisme*, p. 27.   [2] *Evolution*, p. 152.

Mahadeva, the Great God, the Supreme Being. From Him comes the third impulse which is to complete evolution ...."[1] And it is He, Mahadeva, who "sends forth the human Self to occupy its tabernacle."[2]

First of all, let us clear up an obscurity. What is sent forth by Mahadeva in the form brought about by all the previous evolution is a new monad, the human monad. Now, this form was already inhabited by a monad which had been the subject and the support of the progress made on the lower planes. Will there be, then, two monads in man, " The one that had built the human tabernacle, and the one that descended into that tabernacle "? No. " As two rays of the sun may pass through a hole in a shutter, and mingling together form but one ray though they had been twain, so it is with these rays from the Supreme Sun, the divine Lord of our Universe. The second ray, as it entered into the human tabernacle, blended with the first, merely adding to it fresh energy and brilliance."[3] All danger of dualism is thus put aside. The human monad and the monad of form have blended together, and both together are one, and one only.

Where, then, were these monads that suddenly burst into the Universe ? Are they generated the very moment they appear, or have they pre-existed in time. The following passage allows us to have a glimpse at the answer : " The third great wave of life consists of these human spirits which are sent to ensoul and utilise the bodies which have been prepared for them through the ages, through the long evolution, the slow climbing, from mineral to plant, from plant to animal, from animal to animal-man. Then there dawns at last the morning when the human-divine Spirits that have been waiting the time of their advent, hover over the forms that are preparing

[1] *Evolution*, p. 110.
[2] *Ancient Wisdom*, p. 196.
[3] *Evolution*, p. 110.

for them; they are as yet unable to influence them, unable to guide, and unable to control. They form the third great wave of Life that is poured out into the worlds."[1] Therefore, if the divine human souls " have been waiting the time for their advent," it means, apparently, that they existed already before being incarnate.

Moreover, that pre-existence is a logical consequence of the periodicity of kosmic manifestations. The world, breath of the One Being, without a Second, alternatively appears and disappears. It is outpoured, and then indrawn. Now, it may happen, it happens in fact, that when the kosmos is indrawn in the power of the primeval Being, many souls are surprised in the course of their evolution. The kosmic memory of Ishvara registers faithfully the state of progress they have reached. When the next manifestation takes place, those souls come back into existence, and patiently wait for the new world to bring the monad of form to the point of perfection which is in harmony with their previously acquired aptitudes. There must be, indeed, pre-established harmony between the soul and its receptacle. That point of the Theosophical doctrine is clearly explained by the author of " The Ancient Wisdom " when she describes the descent of the human monads :

" Other intelligences .... men who had evolved in preceding cycles in another world, incarnated amongst the descendants of the race that receives its infant souls .... As this race evolved, the human tabernacles improved, and myriads of souls that were awaiting the opportunity of incarnation, that they might continue their evolution, took birth among its children. These partially evolved souls are also spoken of in the ancient records as Sons of the Mind, for they were possessed of Mind, although comparatively it was but little developed—childish souls,

[1] A. Besant, *Popular Lectures on Theosophy*, *Adyar*, 1910, p. 31.

we may call them, as distinct from the embryonic souls of the bulk of humanity, and the mature souls of the Great Teachers.[1] These child-souls, by reason of their more evolved intelligence, formed the leading types of the ancient world, the classes higher in mentality, and therefore in the power of acquiring knowledge, that dominated the masses of less developed men in antiquity."[2]

Let us remember that suggestive passage; we shall find it again, in due course.

So, the human soul or monad, work of MAHADEVA, first Logos, exists before its own incarnation, and, when it is united to the monad of form, it does not constitute a duality, but a single being, result of the fusion of the two monads.

After those explanations, the whole question remains of the specific difference which forbids man to be only an evolved animal. The Theosophist answers us in a word: "Life .... in all beings, is called 'Consciousness,' for it teaches us how to 'know' the outer world. In man, it reaches the stage of 'Self-Consciousness,' or self-knowing consciousness."[3] So the human being is characterised by a faculty unknown to the animal—reflexion. But reflexion supposes thought, that is to say, the assimilation of " abstract " ideas. Hence comes the fact that man is also called by another name : he is " the Thinker."

We shall go on, later, with the analysis of the "Self-Consciousness." What we have just learnt is sufficient for the time being. That summary definition will enable us to introduce, in our description of the Theosophical

---

[1] Let us remind the reader (See Ch. I, p. 12) that, for Theosophists the souls freed from the law of reincarnation can voluntarily submit to it again " for the purpose of aiding in the evolution of the human race." *Ancient Wisdom*, p. 194.

[2] *Ancient Wisdom*, p. 194.

[3] *Leçons*, p. 40-41

doctrine, a very important distinction, which we had left aside, so far, because it reveals only now its value and its reach; it is the famous distinction RUPA and ARUPA.[1] Literally speaking, it means that the seven great regions of the kosmos are divided into two immense provinces; the lower one is the world of the forms, rûpa, and the higher one is the formless world, arûpa. The boundary line between these two provinces is situated between the third and the fourth sub-planes of the fourth plane (mental). And this really means that the physical plane, the astral plane, and half the mental plane belong to the world of forms; while half the mental plane, and the buddhic, nirvanic, paranirvanic and mahaparanirvanic planes belong to the formless world. And it is precisely on those formless planes that the evolution of the "Self-Consciousness" will be accomplished. That is why the mental plane, where either the rupture or the joining of the two provinces takes place, is itself divided into two parts. The name of "mental" is often kept for the lower division, and the name of "causal" is given to the upper one. Sometimes, also, the two subdivisions are simply named by the terms MENTAL RUPA (lower part) and MENTAL ARUPA (higher part). To simplify, and according to the general habit of Theosophists, we shall adopt the first of these two expressions—CAUSAL[2] and MENTAL. But what is the exact meaning of this sort of contrast, of opposition established between the world of form and the formless world, RUPA and ARUPA? Does it mean that from the higher mental, or causal, plane upwards, the Universe is formless? Not at all: "ALL higher worlds are formless regarded from below, that is, regarded by the organs of perception which are fitted for exercise in the lower world; but if a person has developed the capacity

[1] Rûpa = form; arûpa = formless
[2] Causal means mental arûpa.

to respond to the vibrations in any given world of manifestation, then that world to him is a world of form and not of formlessness. Everywhere manifestation implies form, however subtle may be the matter which composes it."[1]

Now we are quite lost! Here is a world, the general characteristic of which is to be " formless " and which, yet, is " a world of form." Do not hasten to speak of contradiction. If Theosophy does not see any there, it is probably because, in its terminology, the word " form " has a special sense, which it is interesting to fix. Nothing is easier: " In the four subtle worlds, the forms are subjective; they exist as ideas, as thoughts only; those are the arupa worlds. They include the plan of the Universe, only to be read by the great clairvoyants; for them, past and future are one and the same, in an eternal present. The mental, astral and physical worlds are called rûpa worlds, or worlds of the concrete forms. Their forms are perceived by our physical senses, or by other senses, called internal senses. Here are materialised the forms created intellectually in the higher worlds."[2] . . . . So, we are told, the contradiction is solved: the worlds RUPA and ARUPA are not in opposition to one another, as what is, in opposition to what is not. They simply indicate two irreducible states of form: here, ideal form; there, concrete form; the first accessible to intelligence, the second accessible to external or internal senses. And we may add that this kind of distribution of the planes of the Universe in two registers is dictated by the conditions which preside over the future progress of the human monad. The " Self-Consciousness " must evolve, that is to say, borrow its vehicles from the ambient environment. But the " Self-Consciousness " is defined by its aptitude to reason, to understand, to will, to handle ideas and to act according

[1] *Evolution*, p. 124.
[2] See *Ancient Wisdom*, p. 112 seq. and *Evolution*, p. 124.

MAHADEVA

to them ; and all that belongs by right to the domain of thought. So, it is necessary for the environment to be, in its turn, an environment of ideas, of volitions, of atoms able to enter into the composition of a "thinking" faculty. And that is why there is a world ARUPA, a world where the forms "exist as thoughts, as ideas only," a world opposed to the rupa world, where forms are concretely realised.

From that first contact with the notion of "Self-Consciousness," we could, it seems, draw immediately a logical conclusion. If the human monad appears on the threshold of the causal plane, that is, on the frontiers of the world of forms, it is because its particular nature forces it to evolve in surroundings where the world of forms has disappeared. In other words, the human monad has nothing more to do with the lower planes of the kosmos. Theosophists do not mean it so. "You may ask, why not give the man at once a mental body only, in which to work out his evolution, why must he struggle through the evolution of this body of sensation ? Because if he misses that stage, he will not be able to make up the links which are necessary for the continuity of his consciousness. At a later time, the perfect man is conscious on all planes from Nirvâna downwards to the physical, from the physical upwards to Nirvâna. On every plane in unbroken continuity of consciousness the Jîvanmukta lives and works. There is no link lacking."[1]

There is not, in the Theosophical doctrine, from a moral point of view, a more serious affirmation than this one. The human soul, the intelligent monad may well represent a superior degree in the scale of beings : before going on its way through the planes which lie above it, and which belong to the formless world, it must descend on to the

[1] *Evolution*, p. 153.

planes situated below, which belong to the world of forms : physical, astral and mental worlds.

Is that sort of preliminary regression imposed only by the postulate of integral consciousness ? The question will be examined later on. Let us be content, here, to point to the capital importance of that article of the doctrine. During the whole of the first phase of its development, the human monad will be united to the inferior bodies ; its receptacle will be constituted by matter taken from the first three planes of the kosmos, and it is with those vehicles, considered as the necessary instruments of its improvement, that it will cover the initial stage of its immense evolution.

But I have just spoken of a "first step," of an "initial stage." There are others, then. And how many ? We shall learn it when we come back to a deeper analysis of the "Self-Consciousness."

The "Self-Consciousness" is made to the image of the Supreme Logos or Ishvara. That Supreme Logos is threefold, as we already know. It is at once Mind (Brahma), Love or Bliss (Vishnu), Being or Pure Existence, or Fullness of Power (Mahadeva). Consequently, the Self-Consciousness, which is his direct reflection, is also a Trinity ; it is triple : " The human reflection of that triple Divine Self is the triple self in man," says Mrs. Besant.[1] But the word " reflection " is inadequate, for, " in essence the natures of God and man are identical."[2] So that there is, in the human monad, a treble faculty in which is expressed the totality of its nature ; in Brahma that monad is Mind ; in Vishnu it is Love or Bliss ; in Mahadeva it is Existence and Fullness of Powers. It is really all that in latency, in potentiality. And, finally, in all that

---

[1] *Evolution*, p. 18.   [2] *Evolution*, p. 15.

there is an order, a hierarchy; for Ishvara's three aspects are not on the same footing of equality; the inferior aspect is Brahma, the mind; the middle aspect is Vishnu, the Love; the superior aspect is the Being. And, consequently, the order of evolution, for the human monad, will follow the very order of that divine hierarchy, which is the one of the successive manifestations of the three Logoi, of the Trimûrti; man will develop, first Mind, then Love, then pure Existence, just as Ishvara manifested in the Universe, first Mind with Brahma, then Love with Vishnu, then pure Existence with Mahadeva. Man will develop Mind on the mental plane, blissful Love on the Buddhic plane, Being and Fullness of Powers on the Nirvanic planes.

Such is, roughly, the "Self-Consciousness," with the law of its progress; a law stamped on its nature, identical with that of Ishvara.

And now, let us come back to the first step, the character and conditions of which we are now able to define; all the experiences which man is called upon to realise through his contacts with lower planes—planes of the form, rupa—have as their object and aim the awakening and evolution of the first aspect of the human monad: the Mind, the Thinker.

First, the awakening. Let us come back to the very moment when the human monad is outpoured by Mahadeva in the receptacle which has been prepared long beforehand on the planes of form. It is important, above all, to make precise the state, or, better still, the degree of evolution of the two elements which are face to face. The monad, compared with the different levels of perfection it has to reach, is all, and is nothing. It is all, since it possesses really and truly the evolutive faculty. It is nothing, since that faculty, having as yet borrowed nothing from the ambient vibrations, remains embryonary. "Everything is there, potentially, germinally, as the tree is hidden within the tiny germ in the seed. This seed is dropped into the soil of human life, that its latent forces may be quickened into activity by the sun of joy and the rain of tears, and be fed by the juices of the life-soil that we call experience, until the germ grows into a mighty tree, the image of its generating Sire."[1]

The "life-soil" is represented, at the moment we are considering, by the whole of the physical, astral and mental planes, elaborated during the animal evolution. Now, however rich and perfect be the vehicles, between these and the exigencies of the human monad, there is a gap, an abyss, almost a breach of continuity. And, indeed, have we not learnt that Theosophists, decidedly putting aside the Darwinist hypothesis on human descent, maintain a clearly defined line of separation between the animal kingdom and the human one. In vain has the monad of form pushed the refinement of its vehicles to the extreme limit of the possible; in vain has it manifested itself in the shape of the highest and most perfect animal that can be imagined; the heritage which it passes on to the human monad is very inferior to the needs, to the capacities of the glorious heir. It is as though, all of a sudden, the organism of an animal were to receive a human soul which would, so to speak, take for itself the instincts, the tendencies and the body of the beast. What a distance, and what a falling off!

And yet the soul must make the best of that organism even if it has to equip it, transform it, make it, in a word, inhabitable. The moment when the two fellow-travellers meet and unite will be critical! And what happens then? What happens is somewhat similar to the shock which causes a spark to spring from the hard stone struck by

[1] *Ancient Wisdom*, p. 129-130.

iron. Theosophists prefer another comparison. The human monad having met the mental body of the monad of form, that body is fructified, "and the embryonary causal body is formed by the union."[1] How does that mysterious genesis accomplish itself ? We are not told.

If it is not given us to understand how that fecundation can take place IN INSTANTI,[2] at least we are able to grasp the idea which is hidden below this symbolism used by occult science. That idea is that the lower aspect of the Threefold-Self, i.e., mind, develops itself by experience. Now, experience, gathered on the lower planes, astral and physical, to be assimilated by the Self-Consciousness, must be transformed into images, representations, thought-forms.[3] But those thought-forms need transposing into general ideas, into ideas arupa. The transpositor is the causal body, which plays, in relation to the data of experience, a part similar to that of the SENSORIUM COMMUNE.[4] Moreover, we shall soon learn that man, between two incarnations, successively loses all his inferior bodies, physical, etheric, astral and mental. If, in its turn, the causal body were to disappear, man would lose

[1] *Ancient Wisdom*, p. 193.

[2] We insist on that expression : IN INSTANTI. Since the pre-human evolution has not been able to create a " mental " fully adapted to the " Self-consciousness," the causal body, which results from the union of that Self-consciousness with the mental is an instantaneous Creation. There is not, in the mental of the most highly evolved animal, the least trace of causal body.

[3] Let us remark, however, that according to Theosophists, the distinction between causal and mental, if it is " very real " is " difficult to define." " The lower mind," it is said elsewhere " is the coarser energies of the higher expressed in denser matter." *Ancient Wisdom*, p. 134.

[4] It is the part that, in the SAMKHYA philosophy, is attributed to the MANAS. But as the operations in question are intellectual ones, the " intellect agent " would perhaps be a better term of comparison. Moreover, all those comparisons with traditional terminology are very remote, and consequently very fragile.

the result of all the experiences acquired during his previous lives, and the evolution of the " Self-Consciousness " would be condemned to a perpetual recommencement. So that something must remain, and survive all the deaths and all the existences : that something is the causal body. To resume : the causal body is the permanent substratum where the results of all human experiences will be fixed. It is the link which connects the Self-Consciousness to the world of forms, and that is why it is as the child born of the union of the monad and the mental. From that definition results an evident corollary : the causal body, permanent entity, does not stop increasing, developing and enriching itself. Always vibrating, it accumulates, assimilates, incorporates the data of the mental body. And it is through that body that the Self-Consciousness manifests its first virtuality, the intellect.

After that, we shall have no further difficulty in understanding why the human monad, united to the causal body, constitutes what Theosophical language calls the Individuality. The individuality, the " Self," is essentially the monad issued from Mahâdeva. But as the " Self " is, during the first stage of its evolution (intellect) absolutely helpless, without the adjunction of the causal body, its indispensable vehicle of progress, the individuality includes necessarily two inseparable parts : the monad, and the causal body. The same notion of individuality appears more clearly still if we compare it with the notion of personality. In the Theosophical system, personality is the very opposite of individuality. The one is permanent, it survives all existences ; the other, on the contrary, is transitory : submitted to perpetual changes, it is destined finally to disappear. " The personality consists of the transitory vehicles through which the Thinker energizes in the physical, astral and lower mental worlds, and of all the activities connected with these. These are bound together by the links of memory caused by impressions made on the three lower bodies,[1] and, by the self-identification of the Thinker with his vehicles, the personal 'I' is set up."[2] "The individuality consists of the Thinker himself, the immortal tree that puts out all the personalities as leaves, to last through the spring, summer and autumn of human life. All that the leaves take in and assimilate, enriches the sap that courses through their veins, and in the autumn this sap is withdrawn into the parent trunk, and the dry leaf falls and perishes. The Thinker alone lives for ever; he is the man, for whom 'the hour never strikes,' the eternal youth who, as the BHAGAVAD GITA has it, puts on and casts off bodies as a man puts on new garments and throws off the old. Each personality is a new part for the immortal actor, as he treads the stage of life over and over again; only, in the life drama, each character he assumes is the child of the preceding ones and the father of those to come, so that the life-drama is a continuous history, the history of the Actor who plays the successive parts."[3]

With these definitions of the monad, the causal body, the individual and the person, we have entered the very heart of the problem of human evolution. What remains will be easier to grasp.

At the beginning, we are face to face with an "incipient soul," an "infant Ego," an "embryonary individuality," doubly embryonary, because of the monad, and because of the causal body, both reduced to the "germinal" or

[1] That memory, as we see, has nothing in common with the causal body. It belongs to the body which registers each category of impressions.
[2] *Ancient Wisdom*, p. 160.
[3] *Ancient Wisdom*, p. 161. The passage of the Bhagavad Gita, alluded to by Mrs. Besant, is in Ch. II, verse 22.

"potential" state. Nor is the mental body at a very marked degree of development. It is only the mental of an animal. Now, however evolved we may suppose it, the pre-human mental is separated from the properly human mental by an abyss. In return, the astral and the physical predominate. The terrible conflict and struggle which are going to mark the conquest of the first progress arise from that disproportion. Unequal struggle, for not only is the "individuality" weak and the "person"[1] strong, but the "formal" bodies, composed of elemental essence, i.e., of particles animated on the descending arc, have an unpleasant and "irresistible" tendency to transform themselves into physical matter.[2] And, while the "Ego" aspires to climb up, the "I" aspires to fall. The astral body, the centre of the sensations, of the emotions, of the desires, tends instinctively to satisfy itself in the objects of the physical plane, even the coarsest, and the mental body, for a long time "is played on almost entirely from the lower bodies."[3] And it is in the midst of that impotency, of that initial chaos, that the Thinker must open his way, realise order and harmony, and constitute his autonomy. Nay more, he must, one after the other, create for himself human organs, for, in Theosophy, the function always creates the organ. The work is immense, and requires inconceivable duration, and would be endless if the Devas were not there to lend their help, on all the planes.[4] The progression is accomplished by a sort of circular movement, which goes from below upwards and from above downwards. From below come vibrations which rouse the mental body to action. Incited to act and fortified by the contributions it receives, the mental reinforces its rational vibrations, and little by little, manages to tame, to submit and to organise its in-

[1] In the above given sense. [2] See *Leçons*, p. 27-28.
[3] *Ancient Wisdom*, p. 122. [4] *Ancient Wisdom*, p. 210.

ferior bodies. But how great is the number of incidents, the memory of which is evoked by that laconical formula ! Let us once more borrow from Mrs. Besant a shortened description of that thrilling drama.[1]

During a first stage " all the experiences are sensational, the only contribution made by the mind consisting in the recognition that contact with some objects is followed by a sensation of pleasure, while contact with others is followed by a sensation of pain. These objects form mental pictures, and the pictures soon begin to act as a stimulus to seek the objects associated with pleasure, when those objects are not present, the germs of memory and of mental initiative thus making their appearance." But the mental images are very transitory. The infant Thinker does not think of forecasting the future according to the past. He obeys his impulsions. " The need of the moment overpowers every other consideration." His morality is not more evolved. For him " good " and " pleasant " are " interchangeable terms." In short, " sensation is wholly lord of the mind, and the earliest mental efforts were stimulated by desire. This leads the man, slowly and clumsily, to forecast, to plan. . . He begins to draw inferences, and even to initiate action on the faith of those inferences—a great advance. And he begins also to hesitate now and again to follow the vehement promptings of desire, when he finds, over and over again, that the gratification demanded is associated in his mind with the subsequent happening of suffering. Thus conflict arises between memory and desire, and the mind grows more active by the conflict and is stirred into livelier functioning."

Then a second phase is opened, characterised by the awakening of Will and its resistance to the assaults of desire, for " desire is guided from without, will from

[1] Ibid, Ch. VIII, passim.

within." Will, in its exercise, hurls itself against many obstacles. The Thinker who uses it guides it "through the reason." But " as the reason can draw its conclusion only from its stock of mental images—its experiences— and that stock is limited, the will constantly commands mistaken actions. The suffering which flows from these mistaken actions increases the stock of mental images, and thus gives the reason an increased store from which to draw its conclusions. Thus progress is made and wisdom is born." And yet the rationalised will has to defend itself against other dangers. It happens that "defeated in the open field, the desires of the personality conspire against their conqueror, and often win by guile what they failed to win by force." It happens also that, "at the beginning of a new mental enterprise, whatever it may be, all the automatism of the mental body comes in the way.

Its materials, accustomed to vibrate in a certain way, cannot adapt themselves to the new impulses." And that is a new source of mortifications and sufferings, further increased by the fact that "when unfamiliar problems arise, as to the working out of which experience is silent, conscience[1] cannot speak with certainty." The solutions are doubtful, and action is too often guided amiss. "When all the paths of error have been trodden, when all have been found to end in suffering, the choice to walk in the way of truth is unswerving, because based on knowledge. The lower kingdoms work harmoniously, compelled by law." From the previous chaos, "there evolves a nobler unity, a harmonious choice of voluntarily obedience, the obedience that, being voluntary, based on knowledge and on memory of the results of diso-

[1] "Will in the domain of morality is generally called conscience." *Ancient Wisdom*, p. 214. Let us simply take note of that definition of conscience.

bedience, is stable and can be drawn aside by no temptation." Then man is ready to go through the third and fourth stages of intellectual evolution. The two previous stages could be summarized in a short formula : extinction of desire. " At the beginning of man's evolution, desire has complete sovereignty, and hurries him hither and thither ; in the middle of his evolution, desire has died, and will rules with unopposed, unchallenged sway." In cosmological terms, that same ascension can be expressed thus : subordination of the physical and the astral planes to the mental plane, evolved and rationalised by experience and suffering.

The two following stages concern principally the autonomous[1] development of the causal body. During the first stage, the higher intellectual faculties assert themselves : " The Thinker, having learned clearly to discriminate between objects by dwelling upon their unlikeness now begins to group them together by some attribute which appears in a number of objects otherwise dissimilar and makes a link between them. He draws out, abstracts, this common attribute, and sets all objects that possess it apart from the rest which are without it ; and in his way he evolves the power of recognising identity amid diversity, a step towards the much later recognition of the One underlying the many." The analytic faculty is thus followed by the synthetic one."

Another step, and man " conceives of the common property as an idea, apart from all the objects in which it appears, and thus constructs a higher kind of mental image than the image of a concrete object—the image of an idea, that has no phenomenal existence in the worlds of form, but which exists on the higher levels of the mental plane, and affords material on which the

[1] We say autonomous, for during the first stages, the causal body has not ceased working in connection with the mental body.

Thinker himself can work." Let us note carefully, by the way, the terms used by the author of those lines. The mental image which the mental abstracts from the concrete world is not yet the idea itself. The idea itself possesses, on the mental plane, an independent existence [1] The abstract idea is only an image of that idea. Hence comes the difference between the Thinker evolving on the mental plane on the one hand, and the causal plane on the other hand : " the lower mind reaches the abstract idea, by reason, and in thus doing accomplishes its loftiest flight, touching the Threshold of the formless world, and dimly seeing THAT WHICH LIES BEYOND." [2] So, no longer does he care much for the life of the senses. " His powers are indrawn. . . He dwells calmly within himself, engrossed . . . with the deeper aspects of life and thought, seeking to understand causes rather than troubling himself with effects, and approaching nearer and nearer to the recognition of the One that underlies all the diversities of external Nature."

" In the fourth stage of consciousness, that One is seen." Having crossed the barriers set up by the intellect, consciousness opens out to embrace the Universe. It sees all things in itself and as part of itself ; it sees itself as a ray of the Logos, and therefore, as one with him. And the individualised Thinker, what has become of him ? He has become consciousness. Henceforth, the spiritual soul can at will use any of its lower vehicles, but it is no longer limited to their use only ; it needs them no more for its full and conscious life. Then, compulsory reincarnation is over. Man has conquered death ; he has gained immortality. He has become "a pillar in the temple of his God and will go out no more."

[1] The mental plane also is a plane of archetypal ideas.
[2] Underlined by us.

Here, once more, all the terms are to be weighed. When man, freed from the limits imposed on his mind by the world of forms and by reasoning, reaches the heights of the causal plane, he contemplates the Universe in its Unity. But he does not contemplate that Unity outside himself, he contemplates it inside himself. He becomes conscious of his identity with the soul of the world. That is the last end to which tended that first part of the evolution of the Threefold-Self. And we cannot see, in fact, how there could be another end for him to attain : now that man has realised his identity with the supreme Intelligence, BRAHMA, the third Logos is "manifested" in the human soul, and the first aspect of the "Self" is fully developed. But it is easily understood that the merit for that ultimate progress cannot be attributed to the inferior faculty which we call reason. Reason stops "on the threshold" of the formless world. It is like Moses who led the Hebrews to the borders of the Promised Land but did not enter it. Reason is an inspirer, it prepares the supreme vision by accustoming man to abstract and to synthesise. This done, it withdraws. The One is perceived by an infinitely higher faculty ; that faculty is intuition.[1] So intuition is the property of the completed causal body.[2]

[1] *Ancient Wisdom*, p. 133.

[2] " Then is the slow process of lower mental, with inductive and deductive reasonings, left behind. In fact it is the awakening of our higher Self and of its powerful faculty, Intuition. Thought then acquires a remarkable strength and power. . . " Truth is known " at a single glance." (*Leçons*, p. 112-113). That precious faculty is not at all in contradiction with those which Theosophy, on the other hand, attributes to the causal body. The causal body is the permanent envelope of the human monad. It is the plate which registers the experiences canalised by the mental body come to out of its initial torpor. A day comes when, sufficiently trained, the causal body can progress unaided and intuitively perceives " Unity."

Is it necessary to insist at length in order to establish that the evolution of those different stages requires a duration which exceeds infinitely the years of a single human existence ? The height of the aim to be reached—the accumulation of the obstacles to be overcome—the brutal reality of experience which offers us the spectacle of a humanity which is infinitely diversified from the point of view of intellectual and moral progress, all that justifies for the Theosophist, the fundamental dogma of the occult doctrine : Reincarnation and successive Lives.

Before making a sketch of the contexture of that dogma it will be useful to retrace our steps, and to summarise, in a short synthesis, what we have learned concerning the composition of the human being. If indeed we want to grasp at once the mechanism of reincarnation, we must be familiarised with the elements which that mechanism is going to set into motion.

One of the surprises which await the beginner on the threshold of Theosophy, is the strange enumeration of all the bodies, which he is told, constitute the human body. He finds himself struggling with a nomenclature of forbidding appearance, including such strange names as: RUPA, PRANA or JIVA, LINGA-SHARIRA, KAMA-RUPA, MANAS, BUDDHI, ATMA,[1] each designating a special body. Why that profusion ? What needs does it answer ?

Our previous studies can spare us this surprise.

Let us take, for instance, an average man, that is to say a man who, on the road, the stages of which we have just described, has reached, not the ultimate degree, but a relative degree of perfection. In that man, the monad, which has been united for a long time to the mental body, has little by little developed its causal body. That causal

[1] *Esoteric Buddhism*, p. 26.

body in its turn, has reacted on the inferior bodies which were transmitted to it by its animal predecessor. Slowly, it has transformed, and put into accord with the exigencies of the rational being, not only the mental and the astral, but the physical itself, the organs of which have had to adapt themselves to their higher functions.

Let us realise the account of those different elements, and we shall already find that the individual we are speaking about possesses four bodies or vehicles, made, of course, of atoms taken from the corresponding planes of the Kosmos : physical body, astral body, mental body, causal body. But if we remember that the physical plane includes, besides the body that can be perceived by the senses, an etheric double, including four degrees which constitute the invisible double of each visible atom, the list of the bodies is increased by a new unit. Lastly, if our average man is still far from having reached the superior planes of the Universe, Buddhic and Nirvanic, he is at least latently destined to reach them. So that he possesses, in germ and in promise, two other vehicles which are to be developed later on by the same mechanism of inter-vibrations going from the monad to the ambient surroundings, and vice-versa. It makes, in all, seven bodies, possessed by the human being : five in actuality : physical, etheric, astral, mental, causal bodies, and two in hope : buddhic and nirvanic bodies. Speaking absolutely, we ought to change that number from seven to nine, as beyond the nirvanic plane there are still the paranirvanic and mahâparanirvanic planes. But, in fact, as we have learned from Theosophists, the two ultimate planes of the Universe remain completely unknown to us. We may in any case, consider them as simple extensions of the nirvanic plane, and therefore, there is no need to introduce a new superposition of bodies.

It only remains for us, in order to justify the above

nomenclature, to place opposite to each body its exotic name. But here a slight complication arises. That nomenclature, which is that of Mr. Sinnett and of Mme. Blavatsky, does not correspond to the notions expressed by the series of our seven bodies. It contains a supplementary element: PRANA, considered as the principle of life specialised in a physical form, and on the other hand, it unites under the same name the two subdivisions of the mental plane. Mrs. Annie Besant has considered herself authorised to alter that older classification.[1] Hers is in fact, clearer and more logical, and is to-day generally accepted by Theosophists. Here it is, with its old and new equivalents:

VII Atmâ : Atmâ, atmic or nirvanic body.
VI   Buddhi : Buddhi, buddhic body.
V   Higher Manas : Manas, causal body arûpa.
IV   Lower Manas : Manas, mental body rûpa.
III Kama : Kâma-rûpa, astral body.
II   Linga Sharîra : Linga-Sharira, etheric double of the physical body ; Prana[2] suppressed.
I   Sthûla Sharîra : rûpa, dense body.

Such are the " bodies " or " vehicles " made of spirit-matter, in which man must wrap himself during the immeasurable time of his kosmic evolution. Thanks to these

---

[1] " H. P. Blavatsky, our revered teacher, expressed much dissatisfaction with the then current nomenclature as confused and misleading, and desired others and myself to try and improve it; the above names, as descriptive, simple, and representing the facts, are here adopted." *Ancient Wisdom*, p. 177.

[2] It was suppressed because life, even when specialised, does not constitute, in itself, a special plane of the Universe. Moreover, as the French translator of Mrs. Besant says, " all classification is relative and must be altered as the laws get better understood and the facts better known." We see in this important example, how dangerous it would be to try and put Theosophists in contradiction with their previous sayings.

MAHADEVA

rapid explanations, we shall understand more easily, at once, the mechanism of reincarnation and the successive progress of the human monad on the higher planes of the Kosmos.

*   *   *

So man, unable to use up, in a single existence, all the lessons of experience which must concur to the manifestation of the Self-Consciousness under its first aspect, Mind, is submitted to the irresistible necessity of successive Lives.

When a man dies, his physical body disintegrates and returns to dust. For a few hours, his etheric double floats around the corpse, then disintegrates slowly in its turn. Conscious life quickly abandons that sort of shred of ether, and alone the desire body (astral body, kamarûpa) remains attached to the soul. But this body is also to be dissolved. It dissolves in a place called KAMALOKA, a special province of the astral plane, a sort of "purgatory," where man undergoes, one after the other, all the transformations preliminary to the happy and peaceful life he is to lead on the higher or mental plane. When he has divested himself of the astral coating,[1] which reduced to the state of "corpse" or "shell," "floats adrift through the astral world" until it is absorbed in it, then begins a more or less long stay in another place, a sort of temporary Heaven, called DEVACHAN. In DEVACHAN, man enjoys the result of all his aspirations towards good, even the slightest. It is in DEVACHAN, too, that "all that was valuable in the mental experiences of the Thinker during the life just ended is worked out, meditated over, and is gradually transmuted into definite mental and moral faculties."[2] There it is that mental images change them-

[1] There are really seven astral coatings, of which the individuality successively divests itself in KAMALOKA.
[2] *Ancient Wisdom*, p. 144.

selves into faculties, into powers which enrich and develop the causal body. The stay in DEVACHAN is proportioned to the number of virtuous acts, the enjoyment of which the soul must have, and of the useful experiences it must assimilate. When that task is done and the enjoyment used up, man realises his deficiencies, and spontaneously decides to re-enter the stream of formal life, to attempt " another experience of earthly life."[1] The coming back to life is accomplished by a movement parallel but contrary to the movement of withdrawal. Coming out of DEVACHAN, the Ego finds again those mental images which constituted the experimental acquisitions of his anterior existence. Those mental images, revived, so to speak,[2] draw round them, on the astral plane, the " karmic material " corresponding to their degree of vibration. The new astral body, in its turn, calls to itself " the etheric double built for him according to the elements he has himself provided, after which shall be shaped his physical body, the house which he must inhabit during his coming physical life."[3] That etheric double is the work of the Lipikas and the Maharajahs, two special categories of Devas. The Lipikas give the plan of it or rather the " mould." They can do it, for every human act is inscribed in a sort of great book of life, formed by the matter of the fifth plane or A'KASHA. The Maharajahs fill that " mould " with appropriate elements, which means that they lead " to the country, the race, the family, the social surroundings, which afford the most suitable field for the working out of the Karma allotted to the particular lifespan in question."[4] We have just used the word Karma—it is amply defined by the nature of the operations we have

[1] Annie Besant, *Karma*, p. 10.
[2] Let us remember that they are to the individual Ego the same as the MAYA of the Universe is to ISHVARA.
[3] *Karma*, p. 44-45. [4] *Karma*, p. 47.

described. The Karma is "the law of causation." If we consider a man's life, we see that some acts, once done, carry with them unavoidable consequences. That datum of observation is extended, reinforced and systematised by Theosophy. For Theosophy, the life of a man is not measured by the short time which lies between the cradle and the grave: it embraces the whole of the time which is necessary to an "Ego" to reach the state of Self-Consciousness. It covers hundreds and perhaps thousands of years, and implies innumerable episodes or resumptions, each of which constitutes what is commonly called human existence. Death is not an absolute term: it only marks a time of stopping and recollection. But it is of small importance that the frame be prodigiously enlarged: during that gigantic existence which is filled by the evolution of a human monad, acts bear their consequences, and those consequences unroll themselves at ease through immeasurable durations. But occult science sets up as rigid law that fact of current observation. The link between acts and consequences is a NECESSARY and FATAL link. And if death did not intervene to put apparent gaps in the tissue of human evolution, and to hide from our view the stitches which link present existences to past ones, we should see unroll itself with all its logical rigour, that chain of causes and effects which determine the circumstances in which every individual is bound to undergo the fate that befalls him in virtue of his past acts. That continuity escapes us, for death, too, is a fact. But that fact does not in the least prevent the law from working continuously. While the soul collects itself in DEVACHAN, its past activity remains latent with the mental images which are the mathematical result of it. After its rest, the soul finds again all it has left on the threshold of the abode of happiness. It begins its evolution at the exact point where it had temporarily left it:

the vibratory tone of its mental body, of its desire body, of its etheric double, of its physical body; the earthly surroundings where it will reappear; all that is strictly determined by the conditions realised in the course of the previous life. One thing only is changed. In DEVACHAN the Self, the Individual, has developed by the assimilation of acquired experiences; its faculties are increased; its powers have been strengthened, it is more able to profit by the new trial to which it is irrevocably submitted. But that inner change will not prevent the law of causation from working rigorously. Man can profit by his new life, he cannot prevent his past life from bearing all its fruit. The principle of *Karma* requires it so.

And man will have to reincarnate until Brahma has clearly manifested himself in the Self-Consciousness on the causal plane. From that moment, which the average man is not likely to reach for a long time, a second stage begins, which will be the manifestation of VISHNU, Love and Bliss. About that stage, Theosophy does not give many details: for, in fact, the more we go upwards on the scale of the planes of the Universe, the less able is the human language to express the marvellous things those superior worlds are peopled with. More than ever, as it is easy to understand, we must leave the description of them to the authorized interpreters of the occult science.[1]

" So far . . . we have been watching the development of the third aspect of the hidden Deity—the development of consciousness as intelligence. Manas, the Thinker, the human Soul, is the image of the Universal Mind, of the

---

[1] " To the realms that lie beyond we now may turn, albeit but little can be said of them that can be either useful or intelligible." *Ancient Wisdom*, p. 162. That is not very promising. The following quotations are taken from Chapter VI of *Ancient Wisdom* (p. 163 seq.) unless otherwise stated.

third Logos. . . While this (evolution) is proceeding we may consider the other divine energies as rather brooding over the man, the hidden source of his life, than as actively developing their forces within him. They play within themselves, unmanifested. Still, the preparation of these forces for manifestation is slowly proceeding." Thence it follows that even on the lower planes, the human being can prepare for the second aspect of his Threefold Self. The awakening happens at first " by the ever-increasing energy of the vibrations of the intelligence." That is the normal course of evolution : vibrations of a lower plane, by intensifying themselves, come nearer to the vibrations of the higher plane. Furthermore, man even then, can already contribute to his ultra-intellectual future," by cultivating pure, unselfish, all-embracing, beneficent love, love that " seeketh not its own "—that is, love that is neither partial, nor seeks any return for its outflowing. . . Pure love brought the universe into being, pure love draws it upwards towards perfection, towards bliss. And wherever man pours out love on all who need it, making no difference, seeking no return, from pure spontaneous joy in the outpouring, there that man is developing the bliss-aspect of the Deity within him." A day comes when that " bliss-aspect " is suddenly revealed, when the human monad has emerged on the fourth plane of the Universe, the buddhic plane : " It is a state in which each is himself, with a clearness and vivid intensity which cannot be approached on lower planes, and yet in which each feels himself to include all others, to be one with them, inseparate and inseparable." And when that bliss aspect of Self enters into activity, its vibrations, as on the planes below, draw round themselves the matter of the plane on which they are functioning. So is gradually formed the buddhic body or bliss-body, thus appropriately termed, for it is a " body of beauty and joy ineffable." And whence comes that joy? It comes precisely from union: "Perfect isolation is perfect misery; to be stripped naked of everything, to be hanging in the void of space, in utter solitude, nothing anywhere save the lone individual, shut out from all, shut into the separate Self-imagination can conceive no horror more intense. The antithesis of this is union, and perfect union is perfect bliss." But again, whence comes that sensation of blissful union? It comes from the fact that the soul has perceived, "in the Self, the aspect of unifying energy."[1] Now, the aspect of unifying energy is Vishnu, "the aspect of the all-pervading life,"[2] the omnipotent supporter of everything, the basis, the foundation, the universal substance, "the root from which all divisions have arisen."[3] So human ascension pursues its unerring march. In Brahma, the soul recognises itself as identical with the universal idea of things; in Vishnu, it feels itself identical with the source of love which has brought the world into being.

There remains for it to reach on the nirvanic plane a last stage, more remote and more mysterious than the previous one: the development of the aspect of SAT, of the pure Existence, who is Mahâdeva, the powerful God: "Last of all in human evolution, is developed the third and highest aspect of the Deity, Self-Existence, the Unity that lies beyond union, and this can be developed in man only because man is one with the eternal in his nature."[4] We see here that Union and Unity are differentiated as representing two different states. Unity outdoes union. And that means, in Theosophical language, that Union still supposes "duality"—duality of the Self and of the beings to which it is united while Unity abolishes all opposition between the Self and the "not-

[1] *Evolution*, p. 23. [2] *Evolution*, p. 22.
[3] *Evolution*, p. 23. [4] *Evolution*, p. 19.

self." So that it is a state where the Self subsists without any limitation, where consciousness realises its infinite fullness. And that is why "the nirvanic consciousness is the antithesis of annihilation; it is existence raised to a vividness and intensity inconceivable to those who know only the life of the senses and the mind. . . To regard Nirvana as annihilation because the limits of earthly consciousness have vanished, is as though a man, knowing only the rushlight, should say that light could not exist without a wick immersed in tallow." Fullness of consciousness, and consequently fullness of being, such is the condition of the "Self," on the nirvanic plane. That fullness of being is of course accompanied by fullness of power. On the nirvanic plane, "the subtlest matter becomes the vehicle of that developed centre, now no longer a circumference restraining and necessary, but an obedient vehicle which will serve when it is wanted and fall away when it is not wanted. And it is written that in the A'KASHA there is every possibility of form, so the life that has reached Self-existence is a being that garbs itself in any form by gathering the A'KASHA round it. Thus it may develop vehicle after vehicle until the whole human series is builded for use, but none of them is prison for limitation; then we say that the man is a JÎVANMUKTA. He is free and all matter has become His servant, to use when He has need of it, to cast aside when He needs it not; every region of the world is His to use, no region of the world is its own to bind Him. He is liberated and as the liberated Self He may if He will still work for His brother men, remaining, until the end of His age, in order to lift humanity more rapidly on its upwards climb."[1]

In such a way does the evolution of the monad end and crown itself. It has successively become conscious of its identity with BRAHMA, Intelligence, with VISHNU, Love;

[1] *Evolution*, p. 160.

with MAHAVEDA, pure Being : the return of the soul to its principle, of the human Threefold Self to the divine Threefold Self, is accomplished. The promise is fulfilled, the aim is reached : " Only as the Self that is God is unfolded within you, will the Self that is the God without you manifest to you the full glory of His life." [1]

*   *   *

On those suggestive lines, we could close the general account of Theosophy, if the occult doctrine did not add to its own conception of the world and of vital evolution a complement that we cannot possibly ignore : the theory of CYCLES and RACES. It is connected with the system, if not by rigorous logic, at least by its spirit, which is in conformity with the profound tendencies of esoteric doctrine. It does not concern, let us say it at once, the ascending movement which unfolds itself on the two higher planes of the Universe, buddhic and nirvanic, but only the transformations which have as a theatre the three lower planes, mental [2], astral and physical.

We learn then that [3] the evolution of the natural kingdoms is not entirely accomplished on our earth, but that it requires the participation of seven globes or planets. Three of those globes, A, B, C, are situated on the descending arc : the globe A, on the causal plane ; the globe B, on the mental plane ; the globe C on the astral plane. A fourth globe, D, our own earth, is situated at that turning point where the involutive arc becomes the evolutive or ascending arc. The three last globes, E, F, G, are localised

---

[1] *Evolution, p.* 15.

[2] Mental is taken here in the broad sense, i.e., as including the properly called mental and the causal.

[3] The theory in question is explained in *Esoteric Buddhism*, p. 48 seq., and in *Ancient Wisdom*, Ch. XIII, and more elementarily in *Leçons*, p. 38 seq.

on that ascending arc itself, E on the astral plane, F on the mental plane, G on the causal plane.

After all, that distribution need in no way surprise us. Is it not, indeed, a fact, that Life unfolds on a planet? Is not the Earth, if we may say so, the floor where Life gets a footing and takes root?

But Theosophy does not admit that physical matter is the only matter. The physical world, on the contrary, is only the outer coating of subtler and invisible worlds. Thence it follows that the Earth, as well as all the planets of our solar system, presents an organisation true to the general laws of the Kosmos. There must be, beyond the physical Earth, an astral globe or earth, a mental globe, a causal globe, that is, a series of globes where are realised the phenomena harmonised with the different manifestations of Life.

On the other hand, on the inferior planes, the vital current obeys two impulses: one descending or involutive, the other ascending or evolutive. So that it is not a single series, but two series of globes which will be superimposed above the physical and visible globe: the first series being directed downwards, the second upwards.

Last, if it is admitted that every form, to whichever kingdom it belongs, has to pass successively through the involutive arc and the evolutive arc, we shall have no further difficulty in understanding that everything that lives—and everything is life—is doomed to pass from globe to globe, before reaching a superior degree of perfection. That circular journey is called a PLANETARY CHAIN.

So far, apart from the idea of globe nothing is very new. The hitherto unknown begins to appear, when Theosophy declares that the vital current, instead of achieving its cycle in one chain, is bound to make the journey seven times over again. Why? Let us remind the reader, once more, that the number seven is an A PRIORI datum of occult science. The only plausible[1] explanation to bring forward, in this case, would be the necessity of accounting for the infinite variety of forms born within the same kingdom of nature. Even in that hypothesis, number seven does not impose itself. However, the whole, formed by seven consecutive chains constitutes, in Theosophical language, a ROUND. And it is only at the end of the ROUND, i.e., in the seventh chain, that the mineral, by means of imperceptible transformations, has become a vegetable. Thus, each vital manifestation, drawn from planet to planet by the kosmic wave, comes seven times on the same globe, with this difference that at each of its returns it is a little more evolved than at the previous stage. And as occult science, as we have said, distinguishes seven kingdoms of nature, it results that total evolution, on the inferior planes of the Kosmos, requires seven complete and consecutive rounds. These seven rounds form a MANVANTARA, that is an autonomous manifestation of the thought and power of ISHVARA. After that, the planetary system[2] enters a period of rest, called PRALAYA: it is indrawn into the depths of the One Existence, until the breath of the One Being, without a second, and the breath of the Great Logos call it to a new life.

Of course, the human kingdom is submitted to the same rhythm. Every monad issued from Mahâdeva goes seven

---

[1] The division of the regions of the Universe into 7 sub-planes could not be invoked here, as the mental plane alone receives on the descending and on the ascending arcs two planets. If the division into sub-planes were applied here, the whole mental plane, including the causal, ought to have only one globe on the descending arc, and one on the ascending arc.

[2] The whole planetary system, with its seven physical planets, each of which is accompanied by six other "invisible" planets.

MAHADEVA

times, in chains and rounds, through each of the seven globes. And that is the origin of the seven great root-races, each subdivided into seven sub-races.

Let us try to show under a more concrete form those rather abstract deductions. Mineral life begins on the globe A, localised on the causal plane, last plane of the archetypes. Having slightly evolved, it overflows on to B, localised on the astral plane. When that passage takes place, vegetable life appears, in its turn, on globe A. When it migrates to globe B, mineral life passes on to globe C, and so on. At the end of the vital emission, the human monad appears on the scene, crosses, as the other manifestations of life, all the first planetary chain, and comes back to the initial globe, having realised the seventh part of its evolution: it is the cycle of the first race. Then begins, always with globe A as starting point, the second cycle, or cycle of the second race, and so on. But we must not forget that, while those evolutions are going on, the vital influx of Vishnu and Mahâdeva does not cease being renewed. Without interruption, new candidates to evolution appear on the initial globe, and begin their remote pilgrimage. Their curves mix with the curves already begun. It is a gigantic gyration, a living and manifold spiral, which, from one globe to the other, throws, over the unfathomable abyss of spaces, liana bridges where cling the innumerable swarm of the beings pushed and ruled by the law of progress.

As to the details,[1] it seems to us superfluous to relate them here. We are afraid theosophy would risk something of its seriousness. Should we not be a little bewildered if we learned that the beings of the first race " had shapeless forms, fibrous, sexless, of prodigious dimensions,

---

[1] Those particulars on the human races are taken from *Leçons*, p. 136 seq.

ethereal forms with at most the consistency of the medusas of the sea?" And what would be the interest of knowing that the bodies of the individuals of the second race were of a golden yellow colour, while the men of the third race— the lemurian—had at first only one eye, in the middle of their forehead, before having two symmetrical eyes? But, who knows? perhaps the prehistorians would be glad to be given information on that fourth race, called atlantean, which flourished about the year 200,000 B.C., and which, before being engulfed in the waters of the Ocean, gave birth to the ancestors of the Chinese, the Japanese and the Red Indians. And would not the European scientists, who hardly dare look for the Indo-European origins before the fifth millenium B.C., be humiliated to be told that 75,000 years earlier, the Aryans and the Semits, issued from one stem, the fifth race, lived on the shores of a sea situated in the heart of the Asiatic continent, at the very place where are now the cold solitudes of the Gobi desert? And could the psychologists restrain a gesture of scepticism, if they were told that the people of the sixth race, which has as yet not appeared, will have six senses, and that the men of the seventh race will have seven? Yes, certainly, it is better to pass over in silence those " revelations " of esoteric science. Such precise knowledge can be but cumbersome, if ever it happens to be confronted with the correct data of science. QUANDOQUE BONUS DORMITAT HOMERUS. It sometimes happens to the good Homer to doze while he writes poems. Let us pass on, and let us describe the last episode of that rather austere poem that theosophy devotes to the singing of the origins and destinies of the world.

There comes a day, indeed, when Ishvara's masterful will decides to make the Universe come back from the state of manifestation to the state of non-manifestation.

MAHADEVA

That event takes place when the seven races have trod seven times the seven planetary globes, when the number is completed of the Elect that were to reach, freed from reincarnation, the luminous heights of NIRVANA. And here is the end : " When a LOKA (a plane of the Universe) rolls up and merges in the one above it, all forms in the Loka just merged disappear, but the consciousness that ensouled those forms does not vanish ; a modification of consciousness remains, a modification expressing itself by a vibratory power . . . and though the forms vanish as the Loka is merged in the one above it—because the matter disappears, being disintegrated into finer matter— in consciousness there remains the power to vibrate in the way in which it had vibrated in the grosser matter. . . As one region passes into the next, this process is repeated over and over and over again, and Loka after Loka vanishes. The forms are gone, only the modifications in consciousness capable of giving rise to similar vibrations remain, until finally, when ISHVARA—whose consciousness was the one consciousness in the Universe, whose life was the one life, who supported every form, who made the possibility of every separated existence, gathers up His Universe into Himself ere he merges Himself into the ONE ; everything has vanished that we know as form, nothing remains save the Centre of Consciousness."[1]

So the world ends. Like a velum, unfolded, then refolded ; like a breath which is outbreathed and indrawn ; like a dream which springs into life and vanishes when dawn comes, so the Universe disappears. Each of its regions, following the inverse order of its origins, comes back into the region situated above. The last one disappears in its turn. It is silence and rest, it is PRALAYA after the swarming expansion of MANVANTARA. And yet all is not ended. How many beings have

[1] *Evolution*, p. 25.

been surprised, by the sudden disappearance of things, no matter at what stage of the total evolution. They have been indrawn into the power of Ishvara before being able to give the full measure of their progress. They are no more, and their work is not achieved. It does not matter! The time will come when the thrill of life will cause the eternal soul of the world to enter into vibration. Once again, on the borders of immensity, the lighthouse of Ishvara's Self-Consciousness will be lighted, and will irradiate in waves of fruitful vitality. Each being will find itself again in the place it occupied when the last Manvantara came to an end. Then each being will begin again its forward course, at the point where he had left it. And the same will happen, again, always, through the immeasurable periods of time which the One Existence fills with its rhythmic and endless manifestations.

We have, for our part, completed the first stage of our work. We have condensed, in a few pages, the substance of the theosophical system. We must now judge that system, and test its value from the point of view of human reason. That will be the subject of the second part of our study.

SECOND PART

CRITICISM OF THE THEOSOPHICAL DOCTRINE

CHAPTER IV

THE GOD OF THEOSOPHISTS

THEOSOPHY IS A PANTHEISTIC DOCTRINE—THE PANTHEISM OF OCCULT DOCTRINE IS COMPOSITE—IT IS AT THE SAME TIME, IDEALISTIC, ANIMISTIC, EMANATISTIC, AND MATERIALISTIC—THE FUSION OF THOSE DIFFERENT ELEMENTS LEADS TO INCOHERENCE—WHY PANTHEISM IS A PHILOSOPHICAL ERROR—HOW MRS. ANNIE BESANT TRIES TO SOLVE THE CONTRADICTION OF A LIMITED INFINITE.

THEOSOPHY, as shown by the very name it gives itself, devotes itself to considering everything, Universe and Life, from the divine angle. It is " divine wisdom," that is, if we understand the natural sense of the words, wisdom that brings back reality to that first and unique cause, to that absolute Being we call God.

So, a critical examination of the secret doctrine could not begin otherwise than by the analysis of a notion so fundamental in the economy of the system.

In each of the episodes of the great kosmic drama, God, as we have seen, intervenes. He is the active agent, always at work. Nothing exists without Him. Nothing moves except by Him. Nothing reaches an aim without being Him.

But if, peradventure, the theosophical God is only an unconceivable chimera, His ruin draws with Him everything else, and the whole doctrine collapses like a house of cards.

Let us render homage to Theosophy for having brought back the diversity of its concepts to the unity of a first principle. Let us even thank it for having thus simplified our work. The esoteric teaching, taken as a whole, will be worth exactly what its idea of God is worth.

This said, let us open the debate without further delay.

* * *

The documents of that debate are before our eyes. We have followed, step by step, from one end to the other, the story of the world, as occult science shows it to its adepts. That narration, all in one breath, so long, and so fastidious as it might sometimes appear, offered at least one advantage. It enabled us to make clear, at once, the master datum which is essential to the system, and now we are able to translate that datum in a few words.

Theosophy conceives the universe, in its whole, in its constitutive parts, and even in its last details, as being only the modification of a reality, of a primordial substance.

Great developments are not necessary to justify that affirmation : a brief retrospect of our previous studies will be sufficient.

At the beginning, "something," unattainable, incognizable, but nevertheless "a real, eternal, infinite existence." That infinite, in order to become active and productive, has to contract into a "centre of conciousness," the Logos. So that the Logos is only a modification of the primordial reality : ISHVARA is the One Existence come to the state of limitation, but substantially identical with the being it comes from.

ISHVARA—limited Infinite—directs the partial manifestation of the Great All. Then he becomes treble. Do not

THE GOD OF THEOSOPHISTS

let us be mistaken about the character of that triplicity; BRAHMA, VISHNU, MAHADEVA, are the same "centre of Consciousness," exercising a triple form of activity. The hypostases that are attributed to them define, not autonomous beings, but the particular functions that the great Logos is called upon to fulfil. And so their names are sometimes implied and their activity directly devoluted to ISHVARA himself.[1]

Let us next consider the specific parts which are to be played by the three Logoi. Have they as an aim and result to put out effects substantially distinct from the agents of whose names they make use? Not at all.

The material planes of the universe, those vibratory waves which seem to spring from the depths of Brahma, are themselves only "modifications" of the consciousness of that Logos. The forms, the vital waves spread by Vishnu are only, in their turn, states of Consciousness of the Second Logos: "He is immanent in every atom, all-pervading, all-sustaining, all-evolving."[2] And the human monads, what are they, in final analysis, but degradations of the divine nature, expressed by the first Logos? They are compared to sparks. What exactly is meant by that term? "In essence, the natures of God and man are identical."[3] Therefore, the spark is not called by that name because its existence is opposed to the existence of the focus, but it is the focus itself, distributed and scattered, so to speak, in transcendental sparks.

And when the Universe has come to the end of one or the other of those manifestations which correspond to the rhythmic spasms of the Great All, what happens? Kosmic planes, monads of form, human monads, suddenly checked in their slow evolution: everything is indrawn

[1] See *Evolution*, p. 124.
[2] Ibid, p. 22 *Evolution*, p. 15.

sentation." Things are only conceived of by the First Cause : that is idealistic pantheism.

We can finally—and that system can hardly be called pantheism—lay at the basis of everything two eternal, independent, irreducible principles : spirit and matter. The Spirit outbreathes a multitude of entities identical in nature to it, which sometimes keep the purity of the divine essence, and sometimes merge themselves more or less deeply in matter, where they become darker and heavier : that is emanatistic pantheism.

Are there other attitudes, other solutions ? No doubt. Nevertheless, if we leave aside the manifold modalities that each of those concepts is liable to receive, it seems difficult to add much to that list. Either the Universe is only the THOUGHT of the primeval substance, or it is its ORGANIC BODY, or its RECEPTACLE, or, last hypothesis, the soul of the world instead of being given at the beginning, is realised in time by the laws of EVOLUTION.

However, that synoptic table will be very useful for our attempt to characterise the theosophical pantheism. As a matter of fact, to which category does that pantheism belong ? Asked under that categoric form, the question would remain insoluble. Theosophy is not connected exactly and exclusively with any of the types we have defined. It belongs to all, and it does not belong to any. It is a composite pantheism.

It certainly is idealistic. And sometimes we might ask ourselves whether it is not idealistic above all. If, in fact, the whole world is reduced to being only the total of the modifications which took place in the consciousness of the Great Logos ; if the Trimûrti and the actions attributed to each of the three subdivisions of the Logos are only states of consciousness of ISHVARA, does it not mean that the Universe is a pure illusion ? The same conclusion is suggested by the part attributed to MAYA in the genesis of Universes. MAYA is the residue of the anterior kosmic manifestations. It is the world reduced to its simpler expression. Inversely, the manifested world is MAYA unfolded and dilated. Now, under those two aspects MAYA is the attribute, the quality of ISHVARA. Therefore, the world, at whatever state we like to consider it, is itself the idea of the great Logos. It is His expressed Word.

And yet that appearance of idealism is soon corrected by other aspects of the system. The revived MAYA is not a purely ideal representation, and we cannot assert, positively, that the kosmic drama unrolls itself exclusively in the thought of ISHVARA.[1] That thought is realised, incarnated in a concrete substratum. The planes of the Universe are neither pure concepts, nor forms which borrow from the atoms of those planes their constitutive elements, nor are they the monads that inhabit those forms. Nay more, even on the formless planes, ARUPA, the archetypal ideas are not abstractions: they participate strangely in the abstract mode and in the concrete one. In short, there is, in the manifested Universe, something more than there is in the ideal conception from which it seems to come. At the surface of the Great All, grows a thick pad of matter, which lends its plasticity to the operations of the supreme Intelligence. And as that pad is united in substance to the One Existence, we are tempted to bring Theosophy back to the long ago classified type of animistic pantheism.

And we should like to keep to that impression, well justified, if the emanatistic pantheism were not coming in its turn to revindicate its rights. And those rights are evidently worth noticing, as several critics have thought right to classify, straightforwardly, the occult doctrine

[1] See *Evolution*, p. 40.

in that category of systems.[1] FORSE CHE SI, FORSE CHE NON. Perhaps yes, perhaps no. Usually the emanatistic doctrines candidly place, at the beginning, the eternal dualism of spirit and matter. Now, here, that initial dualism fails to appear. The Theosophist knows very well whence comes matter. It does not pre-exist, parallel to the One Existence and independent of it. It comes out of the One Being, without a second, and occult science is, as the general expression has it, decidedly monist. All the same, on the other hand, the critics who connect it to the emanatistic conception are not wrong. Does not Theosophy repeat tirelessly that the manifested Universe is a limitation of the primeval substance? Does it not make us witness the successive apparition of those hierarchised hypostases, Demiurge, secondary Logoi, builders of the world, monads, minute elementals, which look like forms issued from condensed vapours? Does it not build a striking picture of those vital waves which, as they go farther and farther from the kosmic centre, become less and less subtle and more and more coarse? Does it not speak about a downward arc through which the monads of form are obliged to run before ascending, degree by degree, the upward and properly evolutive arc? Does it not tell us, also, the descent of the human monad, condemned, before climbing up to the nirvanic summits, to struggle amidst the chaos of the elemental kingdoms and formal planes? Man, an exile on the mental, astral and physical planes, recovers little by little, and little by little, frees himself, recognizes his divine potentialities. He comes back to his starting point, and finally loses himself with ISHVARA in the Super-Consciousness of the incognisable Being. . . And all that is decidedly emanationism, and an emanationism where the ancient gnostics of the East would find themselves at home.

[1] L. de Grandmaison. "La nouvelle Théosophie."

THE GOD OF THEOSOPHISTS 123

And tired of having already followed so many tracks, how happy should we be to stop here! But, alas! we are not at the end of our troubles, and we shall have to add that Theosophy is not free from all compromise with materialistic pantheism, even if we run the risk of astonishing, by saying so, the too docile adepts of the occult science. We are aware that Theosophists boast of reacting against ambient materialism. We have not to verify, at present, whether that pretention is justified. We only want to prove that, in its more general formula, the doctrine appears to us as tainted with the tendency it fights against. One is suspected of materialism, if one gives to understand that the world evolves without directing idea. And, certainly, it will appear that, if there is one doctrine free from that reproach it is Theosophy. According to Theosophists, there would be in the Universe not an unconscious force working towards progress, but a directing thought, a plan, an aim, a willed succession of phenomena. Reassuring statements! And yet, if we make the effort of going to the root of things, we begin to doubt, and we are caught by uneasiness. " Mayâ is prepared in every case by the merging in Ishvara of the whole of the Universe which is to come to its ending."[1] Anybody who has meditated and weighed the sense of those words cannot easily help uttering pessimistic reflexion on the "finalistic" character of the Theosophical system. And his astonishment will increase when he hears that "through the countless KALPAS[2] that lie in front, ISHVARA after ISHVARA arises, EACH AS THE FRUITAGE OF A UNIVERSE."[3] So that ISHVARA is only, in fact, "the fruitage of a Universe." He is the

---

[1] *Evolution*, p. 25.
[2] Kalpa, other term by which is named one of the successive manifestations of the Universe.
[3] *Evoution*, p. 19.

totalisation of the experiences realised during a completed cycle. And that totalisation " prepares MAYA for the following Universe," which means that it prepares the pattern after which the future world will be built. If those words have a meaning, they mean that the plan of a world is not a conception ANTECEDENT to evolution, but a RESULTANT of evolution. Let us imagine a world appearing for the first time. At that first apparition, there is evidently no MAYA, as MAYA is the memory of a previous Universe. Neither is there ISHVARA, as ISHVARA is only " the fruitage of a Universe." And, if there is no MAYA and no ISHVARA, where is the consciousness, where is the directing idea of that first Kosmos ? And it does not matter that the hypothesis of a " first apparition " be never verified. It serves only to demonstrate that the nature of ISHVARA, centre and regulator of the world, is not the cause, but the effect of the world. "GOD IS NOT," said Renan, " HE IS BEING MADE." Theosophy could claim for itself the formula, and by adopting it, the occult science sails directly in the wake of materialistic pantheism.

* * *

So the Theosophical doctrine appears as a sort of " chassé-croisé " through the different pantheistic conceptions. It is supremely eclectic. It takes its material wherever it thinks it can find it. And with these pieces joined together, it builds a system which it believes to be original. The game is dangerous, as it always runs the risk of becoming incoherent. Theosophy does not escape that danger. Its pantheism is decidedly incoherent. From each of its models, it borrows, it takes a scrap, a fragment. It borrows just enough to introduce, each time, in the economy of the new building, a contradictory datum.

Idealistic pantheism escapes contradiction only by admitting that, in fact, all is really illusion. The external world, movement, life, etc., none of these can be anything but the representation, the purely objective idea of a being which, in essence, remains unchanged and immutable. We who profess, at the same time, the reality of an external world and the existence of a first cause, come to a similar conclusion, at least as far as the deportment of the First Cause is concerned. Movement is before our eyes. Consequently, there is a first contriver which is immovable. To that contriver, we attribute the "reason" of the Universe? But that reason, which includes movement and life, is an objective idea which affects in no way the immutability of the Infinite which conceives it. And it must needs be so. God does not change, for, if he were to change, if he were movable, he would no longer be the First Cause, he would no longer be God. In the same way, absolute pantheism, by resorbing the world into the universal substance, condemns it to be nothing more than an objective idea. For, if it is a reality, the Being that includes it moves with it, and the divine substance vanishes in its turn. And that is why, to say it in passing, there are really only two logical ways of conceiving the genesis of the Universe, two ways separated from each other by the substance of the question of the real existence of our world. If, in spite of the protests of common sense and of evidence, we deny the reality of the external world, the formula of idealistic pantheism is the only issue open to human intelligence at bay. If, on the contrary, the external world is real, the argument falls to the ground, we must go back to a distinct cause of the world, which conceives the Idea of all non-existing things, and realises them in its infinite omnipotence. The only drawback—and it is one that cannot be forgiven—of idealistic pantheism is to mix the plane of reality with the

lizing consciousness of ISHVARA—people itself, with imperturbable magnificence, with a multiplicity of monads, monads of form and human monads. And the monad, whether Theosophists like it or not, looks terribly like what we call a substance, that is, a distinct and autonomous centre of attribution, a supporter of actions, of phenomena, of qualities, which is no longer ISHVARA! The human monad, particularly, is not only autonomous, but responsible; it is the permanent substratum of the residues of experiences realised in the course of successive lives. And if we put aside, with a disdainful gesture, the idea of personality, it is to introduce, earnestly, the idea of individuality, which is only, after all, the idea of personality, merely unmarked! We imagined we were listening to BRAHMANAS. We are slowly becoming disciples of the SAMKHYA. But the SAMKHYA was at least logical. To the monist conception of its predecessors, it opposed a frank individualism. The monad, PURUSHA, was no longer the consciouness of the Universe. Merged in PRAKRITI (matter) it disengaged itself slowly, until, escaping that reflection which matter threw on it, it was released and became free again. And that, logically, had sense. The Theosophist, who has not abandoned at all the idea of a unique centre of the Universe, a centre which is everything, everywhere, resides within and without the form, which is, at the same time life evolving and the environment in which life evolves, the Theosophist, I say, who has abandoned nothing of that rigorously pantheistic conception, generously gives back to the monads the faculty of self-action, self-evolution, and consequently denies that they are the phenomenal expression of the universal soul of the world. Each human monad is a "Self-Consciousness," just like ISHVARA, and volumes are used to impress on us the fact that this "Self-Consciousness" bears in itself all the

THE GOD OF THEOSOPHISTS 129

attributes of the great "Self-Consciousness" of the Universe. It is true to say that what is given with one hand to that fortunate monad is taken back from it at once with the other hand. The Self-Consciousness, one day, will know itself as identical with the Self-Consciousness of the world. And this is a return to the pantheistic inspiration of the system. Is it possible to push farther the audacity of paralogism? Audacity, or intellectual impotency? We have the choice between those two hypotheses. The Theosophist, between two seats, sits frankly neither on the one nor on the other. He adores unsteady balance. Has he not given himself the mission of according all the doctrines for the intellectual and religious pacification of all souls? Is not the enterprise above his powers?

Likewise, he is not more fortunate when he bethinks himself of knocking at the door of emanatistic pantheism. After all, the step would be easy to understand, if we could attribute to the adept of occult science enough clearsightedness to have perceived the absolute incompatibility between a system which involves the plurality of monads and an animistic system which excludes that plurality. In fact, emanatism seems to have known how to conciliate the two extremes. It is pantheistic, and it keeps the monads. What a precious help!

Let us say at once, not to have to come back to it, that that pantheistic form is stamped beforehand with a double original blemish. First, whoever thinks himself a philosopher, owes to himself to give one explanation only of the Universe. An ever present idea of unity, such is the sign of the philosophical mind. The world appears manifold. That multiplicity cannot be, for the human intelligence, a normal and primeval fact. Somehow, we must bring the multiplicity back to unity: unity of cause, if we are theists; unity of substance, if we are monists. Emanatism represents the declining effort of out-of-breath thinkers who stop halfway on the road to unity. The explanation of the Universe, is, here, deplorably dualistic. To the eternal mind, the equally eternal matter is opposed, and from the union of those two principles, a whole hierarchy of beings, fallen from their first greatness, is already born. On the other hand, the apparition of those beings raises a delicate problem. They are said to be " outbreathed " from the divine substance. What does it exactly mean? There is not a proper action of causality; if such were the case, what is " outbreathed " would really be a mere effect: and although the effect resembles the cause, it is not identical with it. Now, the outbreathed being is divine just as is the source which has outbreathed it. But if there is, on both sides, identity of nature, what can be the use of those hypostases, with which each of the divine emanations is gratified? Imagination, it is true, will easily represent the primeval substance emitting " vapours," " sparks." Reason will always refuse to ratify that pleasant fancy. The divine being can emit " vapours " and " sparks " only by fragmenting and dividing itself; and what kind of a God, what kind of an Infinite is it, that shivers to pieces? And if he does not divide himself, if he does not fragment himself, he does not emit anything else at all, and the famous hypostases vanish as puppets. The idea of emanation, vague and inconsistent, testifies an intellectual weakness equal to the one that posits the eternal dualism of mind and matter. There is no middle term between genuine phenomenism and genuine causality. Emanatism, an equivocal system, built on clouds and dreams, has not even the resource of invoking in its favour the laws of common sense.

Let us give it, nevertheless, the benefit of extenuating

circumstances, for there is one folly that has generally been avoided by its adepts : the folly of placing, in the higher principle, the direct cause of the downfall of the monads which have sprung, as sparks of fire, from the infinite and perfect substance. And let us even be persuaded that it is to avoid such a folly that they have deliberately distinguished and separated the matter from the first principle. Evil is a fact. Above, let us place good, light and beauty. Below, let us put the abyss of evil, obscurity, ugliness. Let us have the souls " outbreathed " from God's bosom. Let us ally them, at a given time, to matter, cleverly weighed according to the case. Metaphysics is thus sacrificed to morality, but a monstrous error is avoided. The Theosophist, no doubt unconsciously, does not shrink from that error. For him, matter is not a reality independent of the " One Existence " ; it is a *state* of that One Existence. Now, the descent of the monads is, in the true sense of the word, a " descent," that is, the reduction of a power to a more and more marked state of inferiority. Man has to merge down in the depths of the densest and coarsest planes, he who carries the sublime destinies of a being who is to enjoy the indescribable bliss of the nirvanic planes. He must submit to the ineluctable and painful law of reincarnation of successive lives. And whence comes that necessary fall ? From matter, laid out in regions, in planes, progressively and cleverly degraded. So that if matter is a state of the One Existence, it follows that the principle, the source and the medium of the fall is the One Existence itself. Within itself everything happens. It is, at the same time, the luminous emanating focus, and the dark abyss where the monads drag out their heavy and endless existences. In that sense, Theosophy could subscribe to Proudhon's axiom : God is evil. And contradiction is carried here to a degree where it resolves itself into impertinence and blasphemy. The adepts of the secret doctrine will not admit it, I know. May their good faith, blind and deaf, be an excuse for them. At all events, the emanatistic pantheism, already very fragile in itself, becomes, in the hands of Theosophists, a masterpiece of incoherence.

As to materialistic pantheism, with which I have dared to assert that the secret doctrine has some affinity, it undergoes in its turn a very curious transformation. Must we observe that this form of pantheism is irreconcilable with the exigencies of sound reason ? To place at the origin of the world a vague substance, gifted with still vaguer energies, entirely deprived of a directing idea, and to show us that chaos organizing itself alone, progressing from the inanimate to life and from life to man, is to introduce into the principles of arithmetic a complete revolution. No human brains have been able, so far, to conceive the " more " coming out of the " less."

There is, however, a heresy that the " monists " have taken care not to commit. Let us suppose for a moment that the starting point of evolution be an undetermined and amorphous substance. It must evidently be given as such. Otherwise the evolution will not come to pass. If we place at the origin a perfect and infinite substance, the progress becomes useless : we arrive before we start. If we want to progress, let us respect the "protoplasm" and spare it infinite possibilities of development.

Theosophists do not mean it so. Go to the bottom of the idea, dear to them, of a centre of consciousness, soul of the world, meeting place of all the great kosmic manifestation. That centre, as we have seen, does not bear the examination. It is vain and useless, since it is a RESULT and not a PRINCIPLE of evolution. And we remain face to face with that mysterious Absolute which is,

THE GOD OF THEOSOPHISTS

moreover, in any case, the real initial term of progress. So, Universe evolves from something which is already the Absolute and the Infinite. And, to avoid all equivocation, let us remember that the evolution is accomplished, not without, but within, in the depths of that Absolute. And it means that, according to Theosophical logic, it is the Absolute which evolves! Let who can understand. But, to be sure, the "monist," with his absurd hypothesis of an original protoplasm, is more consistent than the disciple of the MAHATMAS.

I think I have said enough to show that the Theosophical pantheism is not only composite but, as well, and chiefly, incoherent. In spite of Mrs. Besant's clever alterations, it keeps the indelible mark of its origins. I mean the rubbish of heteroclite doctrines, taken from all the sources of History, that have been left to it as an inheritance by its first founder, Mme. Blavatsky.

* * *

Someone may object that this criticism does not nullify the main point of the debate. Theosophists use pantheistic ideas clumsily. Are they not on the right road when they look that way for the explanation of the world. In other words, is not pantheism, which identifies the Universe with its cause, more satisfactory to the human intelligence than theism, which distinguishes the Universe from its author?

I have denounced, in passing, the inconveniences, that is to say, the impossibilities inherent in each form of pantheism. I must now take again the problem in its totality, and confront it with the laws of clear reason.

The fundamental affirmation is, as I have just mentioned, the identification of the world with its cause. Apart from that, the pantheistic formula is senseless. If the world is not identical with God, we immediately fall back to theism. God becomes a cause again, and the

on which will break all the pantheisms which, thanks to a remnant of modesty, will refuse completely to suppress what is the *raison d'être* of philosophical speculation. I mean the REAL. So that we can only admire the splendid boldness with which Theosophists describe to us the genesis of that " centre of consciousness " which so fortunately limits the One and only Being, without a second ! But, who knows ? We are perhaps too generous in assigning to them the conception of an Infinite Being, imminent to the phenomenal world ? Is the One Existence clearly finite or infinite ? We know what prudent silence is kept by the masters of the occult science on that Great All " inaccessible and incognisable." And if it is incognisable, how shall we get to know exactly about its real nature ?

The objection is specious, for Theosophy shows, on that special point, a discretion that we shall dare to qualify as unfortunate. And yet, we have been told so : the Principle of things is a " real, infinite, and absolute Existence." And, consequently, we are entitled to treat it as such.

But let us go farther. However mysterious its essence may be, the One Existence does not escape the investigation of cold reason. Is it really the Absolute and the Infinite ? By limiting itself, it ceases to be so. Is it a relative Infinite, in a given order ? Infinite in time, space, extent, and so on ? In that case—the possibility being admitted of all those secondary and relative infinites—it is limited. For a relative Infinite is still a limited Infinite. Conceived as limited, it is dependent on another All, and either that All is distinct from it, or is not. If it is distinct, we fall back on the theistic explanation, and the Universe ceases to be identified with its cause. If it is not so, we begin again our breathless race through all those infinites, which, from top to bottom,

THE GOD OF THEOSOPHISTS 137

are limited and contracted by each other. And it is the same for those "encased" infinites, as for the causes which, in our theistic philosophy, are linked together and rule each other: we cannot go back endlessly from cause to cause. It is absolutely necessary to come to a first cause, to an immovable mover, to an independent Absolute, for, otherwise, the world would never be given.

Only, between the theistic and the pantheistic positions, there is a capital difference. Because the "encased" Infinites are consubstantial and limit each other, the absolute Infinite will NEVER be given, and, consequently in the pantheistic system, there is not, there cannot be, a first cause or source of the Universe. And that means, in other words, that, in that system, the Universe has no explanation, for reason requires, at the origin of things, the absolute Infinite in all orders.

So, the contradiction is irreducible, and Theosophy, even absolved of its eclectical incoherences, falls back, powerless, in front of the mystery it proposed to enlighten. To posit a limited Infinite, is to posit, at the origin of the world, the quadrature of the circle.

It is rather curious to see that that fundamental objection did not altogether escape the rather wide-awake mind of the president of the Theosophical Society, Mrs. Annie Besant. In her book on the EVOLUTION OF LIFE AND FORM, she seems to have wanted to tackle it, at least sideways: "Perfect is the One Existence, infinite, unchangeable; perfect in the ending is the Universe, as perfect in the beginning; why then this long evolution of life with all its struggles, with all its imperfections gradually and slowly transcended? Why from the perfect should the imperfect come forth? Why should it be trained into perfection, and then return into that perfection whence it came?"[1]

[1] *Evolution*, p. 95.

with the sublime familiarity of his language: " Le plaisant Dieu que voilà ? " (What a diverting God !)[1]

But what is the use of going further with that analysis ? Theosophy, because it has adopted the pantheistic point of view, sinks into a contradiction from which it will never free itself. Its God, the One Existence, has no right to existence, because, as soon as he is produced, he destroys himself. And it is not the strange and inconsistent entity of ISHVARA, centre, or rather resultant, of the progressing Universe, which can take its place in the adoration of religious souls. When we, men of the twentieth century, kneel in front of that God, the real existence of Whom is attested to us by reason, before any revelation from above, we are conscious of prostrating ourselves before Him who is fulness of Being, fulness of Wisdom, fulness of Power, fulness of Perfection. And it is because He is really " That " that we call Him God. ISHVARA, mere planetary Logos, fugitive and intermittent focus, even if we were to suppose that he existed, has for us no more importance than has a lost star amongst the millions and billions of stars which people the firmament. And it is that limited God that they want to impose on our intelligence, on our piety, on our love ? We might as well burn at once our incense before the sun ! Well, no. We have outlived that ancient stage of religion, or rather of fetishist superstition. The only Being, without a second, of Theosophy is a defiance to reason. ISHVARA is not God. The occult science has dethroned the Infinite, it has dethroned God. And it is not this science that will be able to give back, to the anxious minds of our time, the right notion of the God of Truth.

[1] Saint Paul and the Christian mystics say, too : DII ESTIS, you are Gods. But the sense of that affirmation is quite different from the sense given to it by the adepts of pantheism.

CHAPTER V

Theosophical Evolutionism

THE VIBRATION, ESSENTIAL FACTOR OF EVOLUTION—SUPERFICIAL AND INSUFFICIENT CHARACTER OF THAT EXPLANATION—THEOSOPHY, MATERIALIST SYSTEM : ALL IS MATTER, AND THE HUMAN MONAD POSSESSES NO ATTRIBUTE, NO FACULTY, NO OPERATION WHICH MAY ELEVATE IT ABOVE MATTER—THE MECHANISM OF EVOLUTION, AS THEOSOPHISTS UNDERSTAND AND DESCRIBE IT, DOES NOT FUNCTION.

IT would seem superfluous to proceed to the examination of the other articles of the Theosophical CREDO. When the basis of a theory happens to fail, all that has been built on that basis is null and void. Now, for the adepts in the occult science, the evolutionist formula depends entirely on the conception of God. More precisely still, evolution, in the proper sense of the term, is God in the making. Therefore, if the God of Theosophists is not viable, evolution, in its turn, cannot possibly exist.

We can, nevertheless, leaving aside that radical vice, consider the evolution as a particular aspect of the system, and study it, no longer in its source, but in its outer development. If we were to suppose that the Universe can be the manifestation of a limited Infinite, we should yet have to learn whether this manifestation forms a really co-ordinated whole, whether the episodes which compose it unroll themselves in an intelligible order, whether, finally, the history of the world, as it is described to us, adds to the general brief of evolutionism

the formal coatings and *vice versa*. The progress of the monads, that is, the successive edification and disintegration of the vehicles, can be brought back to a working of vibratory waves. And if the Universe disappears, if it is indrawn by ISHVARA, it is because the vibratory afflux has ceased.

It would be difficult, as we see, to bring back the complexity of kosmic phenomena to a simpler datum. And we should be ungracious if we were to deny to Theosophists the eye of the eagle which dominates the horizon, and the subtle ear which solves the dissonances of analysis, in a chord of triumphant synthesis.

Unhappily, once more, the secret doctrine eludes the real problem. Its glance is superficial, and its ear perceives wrongly the harmonies of the worlds.

Let us open a dictionary, and look for the word in question. Here we are. Vibration: a backwards and forwards movement, a tremulous and quivering motion. And a backwards and forwards movement, be it quick or slow, has always been classified, in the philosophical nomenclature, as a local movement, by virtue of which some object, globe or atom, passes from one place to another.

So the analysis of the local movement gives the liberating formula which exorcises the obscurities of modern science, and makes it possible to realise the universal synthesis. The world is explained, in the easiest way, by transports, by quiverings of atoms. Surely the idea is very old. It is also very young. It is very old: as early as the Fifth century B.C., Democritus, of Abdera, in Thrace, explained the evolutions of nature by movements of atoms, associated and dissociated in a perpetual whirlpool. And Democritus was lucky enough to find in Lucretius a poetical muse to sing of the marriages and divorces of the crooked atoms.

The idea is young, since, two thousand years later, Descartes borrowed from it the famous hypothesis which disturbed the LEARNED WOMEN, immortalized by the genius of Molière :

"I come to announce you great news. We have had a narrow escape while we slept. A world passed all along us, and fell right across our vortex. If in its way it had met with our earth, it would have dashed us to pieces like so much glass."[1]

The idea is even very young, for, after all, in spite of the scientist tinsel which it puts on, is it not that which transpires through the mechanistic lucubrations of a Le Dantec and through the undulationist dreams of a Basile Conta![2]

Young or old, the theory of vibrations, of vortexes, of undulations has no value whatever, in as far as it aims to explain the order of the Universe.

It has no value, because vibration is not a primordial phenomenon, but a secondary and derived one. It is an effect and not a cause, and an effect determined by the nature of the cause which produces it. The string of a 'cello vibrates at the contact of the bow, and it gives such and such a note and no other. And it would not give that note if, previously, a multiplicity of causes had not intervened ; the matter of which the string is made, and the mode of tension of that string, the wood and building of the resonance box, the quality of the bow, the surrounding air, the artist's hand and the movement impressed by that hand. The vibration is the result of all those united influences, which EXPLAIN it, far from it explaining anything by itself, not even the emotion of the vibrating hearers, for the most beautiful note in the world, which fills a man with joy, makes a dog howl.

[1] *Les Femmes Savantes*, IV, 3. [2] See J. B. Saulze, "Le monisme matérialiste en France."

The receptive aerial of a wireless apparatus is impressed by waves coming from afar. Does the progress of the wave explain wireless telegraphy? Not at all. It is itself, the wave, which needs explaining by the nature of the centre which emits it.

With a hammer, I strike a block of flint. Fire springs up. Does my gesture explain the nature of fire? Not at all. If I strike the calm water of a lake, fire will not spring up.

The astronomer, armed with his mathematical formulas, calculates the orbits of the stars; does he explain, at the same time, the physical or chemical structure of the planet, the comet or the star?

Laplace imagines the genesis of the solar system by supposing the rotation of a primitive nebula. Has he explained the nature of the nebula?

And we could multiply the examples endlessly and take them from all the classes of phenomena. And we should always come to those two fundamental conclusions:

All local movement—vibratory, undulatory, vortical, etc.—presupposes the existence of an object undergoing or producing that movement. The nature of that presupposed object is not explained at all by the local movement which it produces or undergoes.

And this amounts to saying that the hypothesis of the VIBRATIONS leaves perfectly intact the problem of the constitution and evolution of the Universe.

And, chiefly, it leaves intact the problem of Life.

Theosophists constantly appeal to Life to enlighten the deep arcana of the Kosmos. Then what is Life? In vain shall we turn and turn again the innumerable pages where that point of the doctrine is treated, we shall never find anything more than that summary definition: Life is essentially the power of emitting or registering vibrations. To the serious inconveniences which it involves as well—as we shall see presently—that definition adds the serious one of leading us, hopelessly, to a vicious circle. " Scientists " are accused of ignoring the " process " of the life which throbs through the manifold coatings of the atoms, and forms the very basis of all the monads of form or human monads. Very well. " Scientists " will perhaps agree to being converted to vitalism, if they can be shown how the reality of that omnipresent life wrests from the Universe its unfathomable secret. And their wish will be satisfied if one brings them a notion of Life that can annihilate the purely mechanistic hypothesis in which they erroneously delight. Theosophy will have rendered the eminent service of proving that local movement does not give, cannot give, the last word of everything. And here is the logic of the discourse : What is the Universe ?—An assemblage of vibrations. How is vibration explained ?—By Life. How is Life explained ?—By the power to vibrate. Really, who is being laughed at, here ? And if the problem of life does not allow of other enlightening than this one, is it not acknowledging that to live and to vibrate are one thing and that, as a consequence, the total structure of the Universe solves itself in vibrations ? Was it worth while blaming " scientists," only to offer them afterwards such a poor conclusion, and a conclusion which corroborates in such a strange way the mechanicism of our past and present scientists ?

* * *

And there we are compelled by the strength of the case again to take up a grievance that the study of Theosophical pantheism had already suggested to us. Is the occult doctrine free from those materialistic tendencies against which its adepts boast of reacting with a very meritorious energy ? If we follow closely the history of evolution, as it is described by the intellectuals of the sect, the sus-

before reaching the heavy regions of the physical plane? The mineral carries in itself all the promises, all the hopes. It is vegetable, animal, potentially and virtually. Evolution is a question of mechanical reactions going from inside to outside and *vice versa*. The necessary time being provided for, the successive unwrapping of the encased envelopes will infallibly be accomplished. The mineral will become vegetable, the vegetable animal, including the incalculable number of intermediary stages.

Happily, time plays the part of a steadying brake attributed to it, for, otherwise, the absurdity of the theory would immediately be revealed in all its splendour. Let us suppose for a moment that a clever Theosophist has acquired the power[1] to hasten somewhat the march of those vibratory exchanges which are the essential factor of all evolution. Under our marvelling eyes, we should see the stone on the road grow supple, become animate, grow a stem, put out branches, bear fruit. Hardly should we have the leisure to admire this prodigy when, already, the tree would be shrivelling up, softening. We should see it change into a gelatinous mass, into shell-fish, then into fish, then put out legs and wings, walk, run, lump, fly, pass from the flea to the elephant and from the peaceful lamb to the ravishing wolf . . . . Never has the imagination of an Ovid dreamt of such a metamorphosis. Never has the impresario of a fashionable cinema conceived such a fantasmagory. And yet, provided we are given matter, and reinforced vibration, those miracles can become an accomplished fact. Theosophists will probably answer that, nature being ruled by inflexible laws, one cannot forestall the hour assigned by it to each of the transformations of beings. Once more, happy inflexibility! since, with its help, very timely, one can

[1] In the Theosophical doctrine, "knowledge" and "power" are one and the same.

THEOSOPHICAL EVOLUTIONISM

hide the stupendous artlessness of a lamentably childish theory. But the mask is not proof against everything. Is not duration, in reference to the transmutations which affect the nature of things, a purely accidental condition? It matters little whether evolution requires milliards of centuries or is completed in a moment, the hypothesis which explains it is worth what the real causes invoked to produce it are worth. Now, time measures phenomena, but does not produce them. Two factors remain face to face: matter and vibration. Let us activate the latter, and the former will, in an instant, give all the gamut of progress.

And, after all, why should the Theosophical miracle be impossible? Does not the secret doctrine teach us[1] that the JIVANMUKTA, having reached the sublime regions of NIRVANA, possesses the fulness of being and the fulness of power? Does it not add that the Blissful One, conscious of his identity with MAHADEVA, can, at will, don successively, without having to suffer their bondage, the vehicles of all the planes of the Universe? He can, if he wishes, incarnate himself on the physical plane, on the astral plane, on the mental plane. His will is his only law, and this will, we are told, is always subordinate to a work of kindness towards the inferior beings which walk in the lower depths of heavy matter .... If the JIVANMUKTA enjoys such wide powers, why does he not use them to strengthen the faith of the incredulous? If he is full of such benevolent intentions, why does he not come to the rescue of those who, witnessing the miracle, would bow before a demonstration, by facts, of the truth of the Theosophical dogmas? Let the JIVANMUKTA, freed from the inflexibility of kosmic laws, condescend to wrap himself up in a mineral form. Let him realise, as

[1] *Evolution*, p. 160.

he is able to do it, before our dazzled eyes, the spontaneous generation of life, or the biochemical synthesis, sought in vain by Berthelot, and, to-morrow, the world will proclaim itself Theosophist.

Meanwhile, ponderers will rightly think that that formidable evolutive engine, mounted with the help of more or less subtle atoms and of more or less intense vibrations, takes its place amongst the old rubbish of materialistic systems.

But have we not come to a conclusion too quickly? Is there not, in the Theosophical evolutionism, a reality, at least, which is distinct from matter, and consequently escapes the materialistic stamp of the system? That reality is the monad: monad of form and human monad. The monad, indeed, is not constituted by atoms borrowed from the kosmic planes. It is outbreathed by another aspect of the consciousness of the Great Logos. So that its origin is transcendental. It is that which, in occult science, plays the part of a spirit. And, in fact, very often, in the vocabulary of occult science, " monad," " spirit," " soul " are synonymous and interchangeable terms. Is the substitution legitimate? Will the impartial reader be obliged to bow before spiritualism, the privilege of which is so highly claimed by the secret doctrine? The claim is not well founded. That so-called Spiritualism is only an illusion, and that is our second head of proof.

A SYSTEM IS MATERIALIST WHEN THE " REALITY " WHICH CONSTITUTES THE CENTRE OF ATTRIBUTION OF ALL THE PHENOMENA WHICH IT PRODUCES OR RECEIVES, POSSESSES NO ACTIVITY INDEPENDENT OF MATTER.

According to the traditional doctrine, the human being—for, after all, the question here concerns him especially—is made of a spiritual soul and a material body. Those two parts of the human compound, though narrowly united, are distinct and irreducible one to the other. Besides, the soul, although it animates the body, and is the one principle of all the operations, even the material and sentient ones, executed by the human " I," possesses a proper activity. This activity, in the course of our present life, is conditioned by the working of the material organs. All the same, it assumes a character which renders it, in essence, independent of the lower modes of activity. The intelligence cannot work without the help of the senses, of the imagination. A serious lesion of the brains means, for the mind, a lessening, and sometimes the complete extinction of the faculty of thought. But, all things being brought back to their normal and sound state, there is in the operations of intellectual order a sort of plus-value over the operations of sensorial order, and still more over the operations of the purely physical order. The intelligence betrays its immaterial nature by its faculty to abstract, to universalise, to form concepts, and that faculty owes nothing to matter, it belongs to another sphere, to another department of the being. And it is because the animal does not show that kind of aptitude that we refuse it a spiritual soul. The animal possesses only a vegetative and sensorial soul which vanishes with it, whereas the soul of man, by virtue of its independence, manifested by the play of its specific activity, survives matter, to which it is united until death comes.

Let us suppose now that specific activity non-existent, even in man, or non-manifested by any sign whatever : should we still have the right to speak of a spiritual soul ? No, we should not have that right, because, the nature of beings being accessible to us only by their way of acting and by the analysis of their constant properties, it is absolutely forbidden to us to define a thing by acts or properties which it does not express. And, if it does not express them, we are authorized to infer that it does not possess them. Such is the process of human knowledge: we go up from acts to faculties and from faculties to nature, which introduces us, in its turn, to the essence of a determined being.

Now, that total lack of signs respecting the spiritual operations of the soul characterises exactly the Theosophical " monad." No doubt, if we were to listen to the adepts of occult science, we should be inclined to think quite the contrary. Man, during the first stage of his evolution, is called " the Thinker." By his contact, through many existences, with positive experience, he acquires " ideas " and the term of that stage of his progress is reached when he contemplates in himself " the One hidden under the diversities of the outer world." Is it possible to attribute to the monad a more rigorously spiritual and intellectual activity than this one ? In acquiring " ideas," man prepares himself to think the universal " Idea," which contains the explanation of the whole Kosmos. What other sign do we need to proclaim that the monad is nothing but an immaterial substance ?

Do not let us be impressed by that imposing demonstration. Let us go at once to the bottom of things.

If the reader will kindly remember the process by which the monad acquires, little by little, its faculties and its organs, he will soon understand why the magnificent protestations of Spiritualism, proclaimed by Theosophists, cannot impose very long upon any thinking person.

The monad, at the precise moment when it is involuted[1] for the first time, in the lower planes of the Kosmos, is, so to speak, naked. It possesses nothing, it knows nothing. Its acquirements are naught. It is the blank

[1] See above p. 91 seq.

tablet on which nothing has been written as yet. It only brings the weak power to draw to itself a few atoms of the regions it crosses before reaching, on the descending arc, the physical plane, the critical point where the involutive curve becomes the evolutive arc.

Now, those atoms, which it draws to itself, constitute what occult science calls "powers," "attributes": power to think, on the mental plane; emotive power, on the astral plane; physical power, on the corresponding plane. Apart from those powers and attributes, the monad is therefore nothing. And it is by them, and by them only, that it reveals its true nature. "Tell me the company you keep, and I'll tell you what you are." For us, who are seeking to define the essence of the mysterious entity, its innermost thrills, its affinities, its sympathies, in a word, all that wrenches it from its native torpor, this is the only means of realising its deep identity.

But what are then those powers, those attributes through which the monad translates, expresses, exteriorizes its true nature? What is their origin, their structure, their composition? Theosophy does not hide it from us. Not only do they come from matter, but they have no other reality than the reality of the kosmic matter itself. The physical power is matter, the emotive power is matter, the MENTAL power is matter. And that last power, let us not forget, corresponds to the intelligence, to the faculty of thought. So that, on the involutive arc, the monad can only be defined by the capacity to serve as support to material faculties. And we are not authorized to affirm anything more about it.

Shall we be happier, if we question the monad on the ascending arc?

Shall we see the revealing signs of a spiritual reality, of a "soul," appear gradually as the atomic coatings release

the monad as a centre of purely material activity . . . .
We only know, we can only know of its aptitudes, faculties, powers of a material order. And that point, although capital, of the secret doctrine, can be brought down to a materialistic formula.

Theosophists, all the same, with a sweet obstinacy, will go on speaking of " soul " and " spirit." Those terms hide an equivocation. Between soul or spirit, as they are conceived by spiritualist systems, and the monad, as Theosophy imagines it, there is an unbridgeable abyss. No more than the word " God " does the word " soul " take, in the occult thought, the plain and precise sense given to it by Christians.

Later on, on our way, we shall find again Theosophical materialism with its deplorable consequences. For the present, it allows us to restore to evolutionism, which is the chief part of the system, its true physiognomy. There remains for us, to complete the present study, to examine whether, apart from its general aspect, the evolutionism of the Theosophists is consistent with itself, or whether it does not show some intrinsic contradictions which deprive it of its means of action and make it inefficacious. Now, there exist some of these contradictions, and I want to draw attention to those which are nearer to us, I mean concerning the evolution of man.

* * *

The first concerns the part attributed to MAHADEVA in the genesis of the human monads. Theosophy claims not to be Darwinian. " Man in his form " is not purely the result of past evolution : he is " the result of a higher working." No doubt, "*in previous Kalpas*, forms have been evolved, that might fairly be described as half-ape, half-human, that were never occupied by the

Triple Self, and that therefore belonged to the animal, not to the human, kingdom."[1] And if the apparition of man is prepared by the progress of the lower kingdoms, really, it will be the part of the first of the three sub-Logoi, of MAHADEVA, to outpour the human Self into the "tabernacle" it is to occupy.

Let it be so, but is that intervention very necessary? From bottom to top, the structure of the Universe is homogeneous. The spirit-matter, in spite of its differences of density and subtlety, keeps everywhere an identical nature; on the other hand, the divine life (monads, sparks from the divine flame) round which the atoms of spirit-matter group and combine themselves to constitute the forms, is, also, of the same essence. If, in the lower regions of the Kosmos, it does not radiate with the same intensity, it depends only on the thickness of the vehicles which envelop it. Lastly—and is it not now or never that we must remember it?—in the World, not only all is Life and Vibration, but all is CONSCIOUSNESS, for those three terms are equivalent. Even then, we do not see why evolution, following its regular course, could not, of its own accord, and without needing a new impulse, bring the initial monad to that stage where, freed from the limitations which paralysed it, it becomes a properly human monad. In short, the mechanism is wound up. Why could it not reach its goal alone?

The objection is serious. It does not allow of a rational answer. The continuity of evolution makes superfluous in essence, a new intervention of the Centre of Consciousness, ISHVARA, under his aspect of first Logos. And that is why some Theosophists, a little less scrupulously orthodox, draw in a straight line the consequences of the system, and do without MAHADEVA.[2] They consider

[1] *Evolution*, p. 152. [2] *Evoluisme*, Ch. I, B et C.

and the animal should have nothing more to do with the physical plane, this plane having been duly passed. As the matter of the astral plane—and still more the matter of the mental plane—is inaccessible to our senses, that ridiculous consequence would follow that the vegetables, the animals and the men—which are before our eyes—are invisible.

To evade that inconvenience, we should invoke in vain the interpenetration or the encasing of the successive planes of the Universe. In vain could we say, for example, that the " Self-Consciousness " is wrapped up in physical and astral matter, because the astral supposes the physical, and the mental supposes the astral. The answer is equivocal. Yes, the astral supposes the physical, meaning that the evolution on the astral plane supposes a previous evolution on the physical plane ; but, precisely, the passage of the physical atom on to the astral plane implies the giving up, the leaving of that plane by the atom which entered in the vibratory field of the higher plane. The material planes remain, but the atom moves, and it moves in an ascending movement. Moreover, if the answer is equivocal, it is of a kind that proves nothing because it wants to prove too much. In fact, if Theosophists invoke the law of interpenetration of the planes, they will, no doubt, be obliged to generalize and to admit that the form, having reached the higher planes of the Kosmos, goes on being irrevocably linked to the matter of all the lower planes. Now, that is an affirmation against which all Theosophists will protest. On the higher planes where evolution is achieved—the nirvanic plane, and above—the human monad is, by right, freed from the lower planes. Why that difference if one invokes the principle of the interpenetration of the kosmic planes ?

The reader will perhaps observe that Theosophy, having foreseen the difficulty, has solved it in the cleverest

THEOSOPHICAL EVOLUTIONISM

way. Has it not introduced an involutive or descending movement, previous and prior to the ascending evolution ? Yes, certainly, the monad, in course of evolution, does not descend. But it descends, and can descend again on the involutive arc. That doctrinal precaution does not solve anything.

Let us suppose a duly involuted monad. From the moment when it undergoes that involutive action, it progresses, it goes up. Now, either one or the other : either the monad never leaves the evolutive stream any more, and in that case its ascending movement goes on with an absolute continuity, without regression. Or the monad is wrenched from the evolutive push by a transitory accident, such as death. In that case, it will be re-involuted anew. But the inflexibility of the laws of nature requires that this re-involutive movement stop precisely at the degree where the evolution had been interrupted. And, on that article of the inflexibility of natural laws, there is, as we know, no compounding on the part of Theosophists. But if, in the prior course, the monad had gone beyond the physical plane, why, I ask, is it doomed to come back on to that plane, when it carries in itself, inscribed in indelible characters, its right to resume the ascension at the exact point where it had abandoned it ? And if, finally, the human monad begins, by right, its evolution on the mental plane, why is it obliged to go backwards to the physical plane ?

The secret doctrine, I know, offers us a last loop-hole, which has already been alluded to. In order that the perfect man—the JIVANMUKTA—should be conscious on all the planes, from NIRVANA to the physical plane, he must have omitted no stage of evolution. The answer is easy to give, but it supposes precisely what is to be demonstrated : namely, that a movement, self-shot towards the heights, could undergo regression and begin

and spirit-matter, ON THE SAME PLANE. As to the vibrations of the lower planes, they have ceased to be in tune. And here is an opportunity for reproducing another comparison familiar to Theosophists: " Just as a wire will sympathetically sound out a note—i.e., a given number of vibrations—coming from a wire similar in weight and tension to itself, but will remain dumb amid a chorus of notes from wires dissimilar to itself in these respects, so do the different kinds of matter assert themselves in answer to different kinds of vibrations."[1] One could not say it better. But at the same time, one could not better denounce the inanity of a conception which consists in imagining a superior form capable of borrowing, for its progress, from the vibrations of inferior forms. So that the system escapes absurdity only by contradicting itself. If the progress is realised in full conformity with the immanent logic which, according to Theosophists, presides over the transformations of the Kosmos, the stages of the vegetable life, the animal life, the human life, unfold themselves on planes without contact with the experimental reality. If, on the contrary, the imperious voice of experience is listened to, the clever and heavy mechanism of monads, matter and vibrations is stopped and locked: it does not work any more. The occult science thinks it can get out of this hobble with a compromise.

The compromise can seduce for a moment, by its apparent ingeniousness. It gives way as soon as we take the trouble to test its solidity. Superficial in the explanation it gives of the kosmic movements, materialistic in its stubborn refusal to reveal to us the spiritual nature of the soul—powerless to solve the problem of the merging of the human monads into the lower planes of the Universe: such is, briefly, Theosophical evolutionism. It

[1] *Ancient Wisdom*, p. 120

is certainly not in that light that we are used to seeing it presented in the works in which men purpose to vulgarise its moral and beneficent aspects. All the more reason why we should throw open the veils which dissimulate the real basis of the doctrine.

CHAPTER VI

REINCARNATION

REINCARNATION, GREAT OBJECT OF THEOSOPHICAL VULGARISATION—ITS NARROW RELATION TO THE PRINCIPLES OF THE SYSTEM DEPRIVES IT OF ALL PHILOSOPHICAL BASIS—REINCARNATION AND EXPERIMENTAL REALITY: THE PROBLEM OF HUMAN INEQUALITIES—THE DOCTRINE OF REINCARNATION IS AN UNVERIFIABLE HYPOTHESIS—IT DOES NOT EXPLAIN, FROM A MORAL POINT OF VIEW, THE INEQUALITIES—IT JUSTIFIES THE SHORT-COMINGS OF HUMAN NATURE—IT MULTIPLIES PAIN WITHOUT NECESSITY—WHAT CHRISTIANS PROFESS TOUCHING DIVINE JUSTICE.

FOR many people who know it only by hearsay or possess only a vague notion of it, Theosophy may be defined by the dogma of reincarnation and successive lives.[1] In fact, it is under this particular aspect that the occult doctrine gets a footing in the domain of vulgarisation, and that it exerts on some souls a vague and a more or less conscious attraction. One is not tempted, as a rule, to face the abstruse heights where the pantheistic in-

---

[1] The subject has been repeatedly treated by Mrs. Besant and other Theosophical writers. See, principally: Annie Besant, "*Ancient Wisdom*," Ch. VII-IX; *Popular Lectures on Theosophy*. (Adyar, 1910), p. 45-133; *The Necessity of Reincarnation*; *Karma*, etc., etc. G. Chevrier, *La Théosophie, ses Origines et ses trois lois fondamentales: Evolution, Reincarnation, Karma*." C. W. Leadbeater, *An Outline of Theosophy*, Ch. IV-IX. Le Cler, *La Théosophie en 25 Lecons*, 15th lesson. Also the propaganda pamphlets, specially Nos. 2, 3, 7 and 8. Besides, there is not a single Theosophical book in which reincarnation is not spoken of, at least incidentally.

spiration of the system reveals itself. Willingly, too, and by virtue of the same law of the least effort, one leaves aside the speculations of Theosophists on the complicated mechanism of the Universe. With reincarnation, on the contrary, curiosity is awakened, and stirs up a sense of competence. On the whole, the theory presents itself upheld by easily grasped reasons. It appeals to the deepest instincts of the human being : Instinct of justice, instinct of happiness, instinct of survival. To weak Christians whose faith is wavering, it opens, on the sanctions of the next world, reassuring perspectives. In short, it brings an answer to that kind of problem which the common mortal discusses and solves, a little at random, under the impulse of individual preferences. So that we must give it a very special attention.

Besides, Theosophists seem to have understood that the future of their sect was linked with the success obtained, in the mind of the public, by that chapter of their teaching. For once, they deign to come into contact with experience. According to them, human life becomes an undecipherable enigma, if it is not enlightened by the doctrine of reincarnation. For once, too, they deign to reduce as much as possible the exotic and strange terminology which usually encumbers their works. Apart from two or three expressions, indispensable by the way, such as KARMA, KAMALOKA, DEVACHAN,[1] they try to speak a clear and explicit language. If we were not duly warned, we could, by and by, begin to believe that reincarnation forms, in the occult science, a sort of inlock which justifies itself, and has, so to speak, no need of being joined to the general lines of the system.

It is probably thought that, if victory be won on that point, there will always be time to lead the new adepts to the sanctuary where the profound doctrine wraps itself

[1] On the general mechanism of reincarnation, see above, ch. III.

up in the veils of sacred terminology. The doctrine of reincarnation is the fathom line and the bait which are used to attract proselytes. That is another reason for studying it carefully. However, we shall be careful to avoid the trap laid for the credulity of the ignorant. Certainly, we shall follow Theosophy, since it deigns to condescend to it, on the ground of experience, from which it boasts of borrowing its more victorious arguments. But we shall take care not to forget that the dogma of successive lives is linked to the whole of the system, of the first principles of which it is only an application.[1]

* * *

To tell the truth, if we had to be satisfied with the use of that logic which consists in judging the value of conclusions by the value of principles, the case would be won already. Why is man submitted to the law of reincarnation? The real reason, the only reason invoked by Theosophists, is taken from the immensity of the work we should have to accomplish before reaching the goal fixed for us by nature. Starting from the borders of animality, the human monad must become conscious of its identity with the supreme intelligence whence the Universe proceeds. The distance between the starting point and the aim is too great to be covered in the interval of one existence: " Looking at man as we see him in this life, with the small span of years that comes between the first cry of the babe and the last sigh of the dying, so brief a time and with so much to do, so vast a task and so short a span—a work so great must need a method extended and rational, for the whole world is rational, being ordered

---

[1] Such is, besides, the formal teaching of Mrs. Besant : " The reincarnation of the human soul is not the introduction of a new principle into evolution, but the adaptation of the universal principle to meet the conditions rendered necessary by the individualizations of the continuously evolving life." *Ancient Wisdom*, p. 179.

REINCARNATION

by the supreme Wisdom, as well as sustained by infinite Love."[1] The strength of the argument is increased if we consider the enormous duration of time needed for the evolution of inferior beings. How many diversified and linked forms have had to be donned by the formal monad before it reaches the level of simple animal life![2] Think of the stupendous accumulation of centuries and millenia required for the atoms of coarse matter to be changed into atoms gifted with sensibility! Add to it the long and mysterious push which causes the species to evolve from one to the other. Finally, ask the scientists what they think of the duration of geological times, and you will have an approximate idea of the unending slowness with which nature has written the introduction to the human evolution!

And, if the introduction is so long, what about the book! And as—we have seen it—the monad issued from MAHADEVA is carried away by the same stream of vibrations which carries the monads of form; as it must, little by little, edify and build, with the atoms borrowed from the material surroundings, its body, its physical organs, its brains, its sensitive and mental faculties, the laws of its evolution are exactly the laws of the evolution of forms. So, the development of the human monad participates in the majestic slowness which characterises the manifestation of the supreme Logos. And what are the thirty or forty years which represent the average human life, as opposed to that formidable delay? A drop of water in the ocean. The formal monad has been incarnated and reincarnated thousands and thousands of

---

[1] *Popular Lectures*, p. 44.
[2] Let us note, in passing, that Theosophists grant the lower species only a "specific monadic group-soul." "Individuality" is intimated only in the more evolved species. See *Ancient Wisdom*, p. 189.

times before emerging on the level of the mental plane. The human monad will be incarnated and reincarnated thousands and thousands of times before emerging at the level of the Buddhic plane.[1] So that reincarnation is a rigorous and irresistible consequence of the general principles of the Theosophical system, even before being, as we are told, a postulate of true experience.

All this would be very impressive, if the general principles of the Theosophical system were true. Reincarnation would perhaps impose itself, if the goal of the present life was, for man, to become conscious of his substantial identity with the universal life of the world. Humanity, in the course of the forty or fifty millenia it is said to have already spent on earth, not having acquired the feeling of such an identity, and not appearing to be on the point of acquiring it, we could conclude that, on pain of being frustrated in its natural end, it is reincarnated to obey the law of immanent justice. But first, the demonstration would have to be made that such is, in fact, the aim of human life. One would have to demonstrate that the many "personalities," the numberless "egos" which constitute, through centuries, the

[1] There was a time when Theosophists tried to calculate the probable number of the incarnations of the monad taking place during the occupation of any planet by the human life-wave. Mr. Sinnett (*Esoteric Buddhism*, p. 145), who makes these calculations, says that "if one existence only be passed by the monad in each of the branch races through which it must pass at least once, the total number accomplished during a round period on one planet, would be 343, the third power of 7." Really, we must estimate, at least, the number of existences which each man must pass through in the course of a single kosmic manifestation to be 800 .... if everything takes place as it should. But how many accidents there are to foresee, how many delays, due to the working of the law of KARMA! The more modern Theosophists refrain from giving even approximate numbers.

human family, are to be melted one day into one solitary personality. It would be necessary, in a word, for pantheism to be the only viable explanation of the world. Now, pantheism is an error. Consequently, reincarnation is not imposed on us.

And if, ignoring the first and irreducible inconvenience, we reintegrate—and we have a right to do so—the mechanism of reincarnation in the general mechanism of kosmic evolution, the impossibilities of the one denounce the impossibilities of the other. Reincarnation would be conceivable if man were, to such a degree as Theosophists assert, the slave of the kosmic planes and whirlpools which surround and pervade him. Let us admit, for a moment, that the universe is ruled according to the formula of vibratory movements we have already mentioned. In that hypothesis, the human monad owes everything to the kosmic atmosphere wherein it is merged : not only the elements of its physical body and the organs of that body, but also its sensations, its ideas, its mental faculties. From his eyes, which contemplate the outer world, to his intelligence, which conceives thought, man is matter, he is only matter. If such is the case, the human evolution is conditioned by the kosmic evolution and his Self is the fruitage of it, as ISHVARA is the fruitage of a complete universe. And as the transformations of matter are accomplished with infinite slowness, it follows that man, too, evolves very slowly. He will never pass the line which marks the front of the material wave wherein he is merged. He is in the ranks. He cannot get out of it, not even by death, which is not able to break the rigid necessity of fate. So that he must be born again to take his place once more in the anonymous flood which calls for him. [1]

---

[1] All the same, death, in the Theosophical system, is a very strange fact, very difficult to explain. If, indeed, evolution is

And the reasoning would be just, if it were true that the human being is nothing and is able to do nothing except through the matter which dominates him, far from his being its master. The reasoning would be worth listening to, if man did not possess, outside and above matter, that SOMETHING which frees him, in some measure, and which is called mind—I mean the immaterial mind. It is because he possesses that mind that man is capable of conceiving the absolute, without being obliged to go through the unending cycle of an experience which, moreover, would never give him the notion of the absolute, if intelligence had not the privilege and the power of transposing the data of experience into truths, into principles valid in all past, present and future cases. It is because he possesses that mind, that man can discern, as soon as he is truly a man, good from evil, and can conform his life, his activity, to all that is presented to him in the light of conscience and duty. And it is, finally, because he possesses that mind, that man—his whole history is there to bear witness to it—can outstrip, like a swift and bounding steed, the slow progress of material evolution. While around him the world seems to mark time and to be shut in a cycle of inexorable laws, he goes, his head held high, enslaving to his energy the forces of nature, taming elements, pushing his way amid the necessity which presses him on all sides, opening round him vistas and glades of freedom. Any civilization, however humble and miserable

CONTINUOUS, why those sudden gaps, why those sudden breaks, why that hurried disintegration of physical atoms? Physical matter also, ruled by the law of vibratory movements, ought to change very gradually without shocks, without break. If we really think it over, we shall see that there is no fact more incompatible with the Theosophical doctrine than the fact of death. But, on that point, as on many others, the occult science must needs bow before brutal reality, to which is adapted, come what may, a PRECONCEIVED hypothesis.

it may be imagined at its beginning, is a victory of man over the coercion exercised by the brutal realities of matter. Often, in that gigantic struggle, man is defeated, either when he struggles with matter outside himself, or when he struggles with matter inside himself. But often, too, he is triumphant, and, if he triumphs, it is because his face is illumined with a splendour which is not the splendour of matter, but the light of intelligence and the power of will. Therefore if man, owing only to the fact that he is man, possesses, at every degree, at every moment of his history, that double nobility, we are allowed to conclude—and we do not want, at present, to conclude more—that there can exist another solution to the problem of destiny than reincarnation, a solution that does not suppose the absolute control of matter over human progress.

If only evolution, interpreted in that sadly materialistic sense, were coherent, the occult science could try to dispute with criticism the dogma of successive lives. Let us be conciliatory to the very end. Let us suppose that man reincarnates himself in the hope of one day identifying his consciousness with the consciousness of the Universe. Let us suppose that to reach that goal he has to borrow his means of progress from vortexes of atoms which drag him in the gigantic spiral of chains, rounds and planetary cycles. It is at least necessary for all that mechanism to be able to work. Now, it happens, precisely, that the wheels, round which twine the human clusters, anxious to reincarnate themselves, do not work. When, in the previous chapter, we demonstrated the contradictions inherent to the descent of the human monad on the planes lower than the causal one, we might have added, already, that the Theosophical idea of reincarnation was struck with sterility. In order that man may be reincarnated, it is necessary for him to be able to evolve through the

Besant's pen describes with striking realism.[1] He has only bad examples before his eyes. Hardly has he reached the age of reason, when he is employed for base and ignoble tasks. He becomes depraved. He is given to vice. He becomes a thief. He is put into prison. He comes out of it more degraded than before. One day, he commits a murder. Tired of him, society sends him to the scaffold or to the guillotine. Really and truly, has that criminal deserved his earthly fate, and the eternal one that, in addition, Christianity attributes to him? Was he not predestined to evil? Why that predestination? Now, a little further away, another child is born. He opens his eyes to the light, and everything smiles upon him, honourable family, fortune, attentive care, refined education : he lacks nothing of what may lead him to happiness. Moreover, nature seems to have delighted in loading him with its favours : a straight character, a clear intelligence, a firm will, perfect health. The child, when a young man, will become a model of work and virtue. He belongs to the race of geniuses or saints. He will be the glory of the country where he was born. He was, so to speak, predestined to good. In what respect, more than the child who is a disinherited and a criminal by vocation, has he deserved his fate? And whence comes the fact that the God of all justice and all kindness has created such a gulf between those two children?

Another aspect of the problem : To anyone who wants to study it rather closely, social progress seems conditioned by the development of an indispensable quality : altruism, i.e., self-abnegation, self-sacrifice. Parents devote themselves to their children, citizens to their country; heroes walk to death to save their fatherland. Profiteers, ambitious men, tyrants even would never realise their ambitions if they were not helped and served, in one way or

[1] *Popular Lectures*, p. 67 seq.

another, by the anony mous disinterestedness of the honest people who uphold the framework of the society to which they belong. Now, is it not a fact of experience that not only altruism hardly ever receives the reward it deserves in all justice, but that, often, men devoted to the common good perish under their task, and die before they have been able to complete their beneficent work ? They disappear. The world ignores or forgets the sublime lessons given by their noble conduct. It goes on its way, careless, ungrateful and selfish, so that, according to every reasonable prevision, society, deprived of its strongest upholders, ought, sooner or later, to degenerate and disappear. And yet society does not disappear. How is it that the fountain of self-sacrifice is never dried up ? Why, considering that almost invariably the good people are the victims of the bad ones, does good persist in pursuing, in spite of so many obstacles and rebuffs, its silent conquests, which are effectual, after all, since social progress itself is also a fact ?

To that first group of questions, which are amongst the most perplexing over which the mind of man, especially of the modern man, has pondered, reincarnation brings a victorious answer. No, even the roughest savage, even the most barbarous man, is not a wretch, that the so-called justice of a heartless God has doomed to vegetate hopelessly in ignorance and bestiality. No, the child who is born in the ignoble slums of our great cities is not a criminal doomed to undergo the punishment of vices and crimes for which he is not responsible. Those poor creatures whose fate on earth and after death wrings from us a cry of indignation and of pity, are not what they seem to be. We look upon them as degenerate, full of ignominy ? Let us forget our prejudices for a moment, and enlarge our paltry horizons. Let us glance at the immense procession of souls carried by the stream of kos-

tary murder committed in another life. To atone for the blunder of which he has been guilty, he loses, in being reincarnated for nothing, a turn of evolution. Why, again, do some people come into the world afflicted with physical deformities? They were, previously, tormentors: wild Inquisitors, exercising their fanatical rage on innocent persons; or vivisectors immolating, to the so-called necessities of science, poor defenceless beasts. Nature avenges victims; it causes their torturers to be re-born as invalids. Why, again—and we cannot quote all— why do two beings, put face to face by the chances of life, feel towards each other a sympathy or an antipathy that nothing can explain? Those two beings, in fact, are not unknown to each other. In the course of a past existence, they loved or hated each other. They find each other again, and hatred as well as love is manifested here by love at first sight, there by an insurmountable aversion.

Such are the principal facts which, according to Theosophists, posit the theory of reincarnation: " Reincarnation makes all life intelligible; a flood of light pours over human life, and we can see it in its inception, its evolution and its goal."[1]

Is that true? Before deciding, it would be well to call attention again to the fundamental notion which constitutes the key-stone of Theosophical reincarnation. That central notion is that of KARMA.[2] The KARMA, or law of causation, is only a particular application of the inflexible rigidity of natural laws. " When one thing has happened, another definite thing invariably follows it."[3] Place your hand above a flame: infallibly, your hand will be burnt. Throw a stone on to a window pane: infallibly

[1] *Popular Lectures*, p.49
[2] See above, p. 102.
[3] *Popular Lectures*, p. 104.

the glass will be broken. Now, that rigorous linking of
effects to causes is verified also in the moral order, according to the principles of occult science.[1] Given such
and such an act, the consequence will infallibly follow.
Good calls for good. Evil calls for evil. Multiply those
acts, good or bad, and, little by little, your individuality
will be laden with a more or less heavy burden of causes
which, sooner or later, will produce their effects. They
will not necessarily produce them in the course of a single
existence. Such a short time is not sufficient to use up
the totality of consequences required by the antecedents.
No matter. You will lose nothing by waiting. Your
capital will cling to you, and will accompany you until
the day when it will have given all its fruits. Such is
KARMA, by virtue of which every debt is paid, and every
virtue receives, even on earth, its reward. Through it,
moral balance is established or re-established through the
series of successive lives. It is useless to underline, by
examples, this point of the secret doctrine. We should
have to return to each of those we gave a moment ago.
Let us be content to register the three subsidiary laws
under the general law of action:[2] " Thought is the power
that builds up character; as you think, you will be.
The force which we call desire or will .... draws together
the things you desire .... The effect of your conduct
upon others, causing them happiness or misery, brings
you happiness or misery in return."[3] This being given,

---

[1] A necessary assimilation, in a system where matter is all. A
contestable assimilation, in a system where the spiritual faculties of
the soul are taken account of.

[2] *Popular Lectures*, p. 110.

[3] To give only one example, Mrs. Annie Besant imagines the
" savage " in a rather rudimentary way. She could, with advantage,
complete her documentation by consulting works of scientific
ethnology. Has she taken the trouble to read about those Australians, of which she draws such a pitiful picture, the reports of ex-

eludes the difficulty, but it does not solve it. The better we demonstrate to man that he is unable to realise the memory of his past lives, the more problematic also will the EXPERIMENTAL verification of reincarnation become. And be that as it may concerning abstract theories, we shall remain face to face with the brutal fact: we do not know whether we have already existed.

I shall go farther. If it is admitted that, in DEVACHAN, acts are transmuted into faculties, does it follow that we are forbidden to keep any recollection of past existences? Not at all. By means of accumulating certain kind of acts, I contracted a habit. For instance, I learned a foreign language. Surely, I would not be able to remember, in all their peculiar circumstances, all the efforts I made, all the steps I took to learn that language. There is, all the same, a fact I remember perfectly: it is that I learned that language at a certain time of my life. In short, we know how to assign, to a moment of time, certain modifications occurring in the structure of our soul, even if we cannot reconstitute the series of acts which generated them. So that if, in DEVACHAN, or elsewhere, we contracted a new tendency, we ought to have at least the recollection, confused and vague, but alive, of those deep transformations which took place in our being. THE TENDENCY ITSELF WOULD SPEAK OF ITS ORIGINS. Now, this tendency does not speak. It is given, when consciousness awakes, as a brutal and anonymous fact, without link with our personal past. In vain could we object that, in his new existence, man wraps himself up in entirely new inferior bodies: mental, astral, physical.[1] It is true none the less that, according to Theosophists, the tendency is impressed in these bodies, and so deeply that it determines their form. Therefore those bodies are in relation to it, they can, they ought to know it, and

[1] See *Popular Lectures*, p. 96.

if they know it, why do they learn nothing, even confusedly, of its origins? Why, in other words, have we not something like a foreboding, like a vague apprehension, a last vestige of past lives?[1]

Theosophists themselves feel the need of getting out of that difficulty. After having shown us why we do not remember, they coldly add that it is perfectly possible for us to remember. "I know," says Mrs. Besant, "a very fair number of people who can remember, who can compare notes, and verify facts, and recognise one another through the millenia of the past."[2] The best answer to oppose to these curious exceptions is given us by Mrs. Besant herself: "To each who has done it this is the best of all proofs. But it is no proof to another."[3] And this is true. Anybody will be able to tell us, like Dr. Lucien Graux,[4] for instance, the romance of his past lives. He will proclaim himself "Reincarnate" or "Haunted" and will find people simple-minded enough to believe his confidences. Really, stories of that kind have no scientific value, because there are no rational means of controlling them. And then, how is it that our memories, duly condensed into "tendencies" and having, therefrom, lost the clernaess of their outline, can nevertheless be found again, as clear, as precise as on the day when they were registered on earth? We are told that the eternal and permanent "Self" keeps them in that condition.[5] The reason is bad. Is not the "Self" the monad wrapped up in the causal body, and is not the causal body precisely the focus where the acquired experiences are blended together, in DEVACHAN, to give birth to the faculties?

---

[1] As we remember vaguely, although Mrs. Besant denies it, having "learnt how to read" when we were at school.
[2] *Popular Lectures*, p. 99.   [3] Ibid.
[4] Author of a book entitled *Réincarné*.
[5] *Popular Lectures*, p. 97.

increasing progress, and this indefinitely and without anyone being able to set a term to the eternal evolution, in a world where God himself—call that God ISHVARA, Logos, it does not matter—is only the ever-increased totalisation of the experiences realised in the course of successive MANVANTARAS, where then is the stable and immutable centre, whence could emanate the absolute verdict which says : " This is Good ; this is Evil " ? Do not speak of the " Super-Consciousness." It does not play any active part in the Kosmos, and it is, moreover, out of reach, incognisable. Everything moves, walks, changes, in us, around us, above us ; the moral of tomorrow will not be the moral of to-day ; the moral of a future ISHVARA will not be that of the ISHVARA who is supposed to rule us. No absolutism, no law. Theosophy has no right to speak those words, alien to the innermost structure of its doctrine.

Nor has it the right to speak of free-will. In a world where all is matter, where man is nothing and can do nothing, except by matter—coarse or subtle, it makes no difference—in a world where the idea itself, which is, after all, the root of freedom, cannot, because of its identification with matter, embrace the horizons of the eternal, of the abstract, of the absolute, there is no place for freedom. And I insist on that point. Why is man free ? Because he can conceive the absolute, and because, the absolute never being realised by the poor earthly goods, he is capable of choosing or of not choosing such and such of those goods which, in the world, cannot fulfil his need of the infinite. Suppress the idea—that door opened on the infinite, and through which the breath of liberty penetrates into our soul—and man becomes a slave to his lower instincts, to his appetites of the moment. The horizon closes in front of him, and he goes on, with head bent towards the earth, groping his way in a narrow,

REINCARNATION

limited world, which carries him in its breathless and anonymous course, towards an unknown goal. In materializing the idea, Theosophy has killed freedom, just as, in proclaiming the eternal making of things, it has killed law. On principle and by right, moral law is excluded from the Theosophical perspective. And as reincarnation is only a particular case, an aspect of the Universal evolution, it has nothing to do with the moral problem. Man reincarnates because the world is in the making: nothing more.

If such is the case, the doctrine of successive lives must betray its congenital powerlessness by internal vices which will completely enlighten us on the so-called moral reach to which it aspires. These vices are easy to discover.

There is a critical moment in the history of human evolution. It is when the monads are incarnated for the first time. We are allowed to contemplate this moment, since the apparition of human monads on the mental plane is posterior to the organization of the kosmic planes by BRAHMA and the evolution of forms under the impulse of VISHNU.[1]

And we dare put that question: when they incarnate for the first time, are the monads equal or unequal? If they are equal, the previous evolution having been accomplished in a uniform and continuous way, all the animal receptacles which are to receive them, have reached exactly the same level of development. In that hypothesis, the individual evolution of each human monad will

---

[1] And even if we were to admit that part of the animal kingdom passed, in olden times, into the human kingdom there must have been a certain moment when animal evolution itself began, and, as that animal evolution prepares human evolution, the terms of the problem of origins, in that hypothesis, are not suppressed, but only removed.

thereafter show no difference from the other monads. The conditions are exactly the same for all of them. The law of evolution will be set into motion and will play, as before, in a uniform and continuous way. The progress will be parallel and will present no difference between one monad and another. Any difference, indeed, would mean that the evolutive law has played deficiently: an unlikely circumstance, and one for which, at any rate, man could not be held responsible. If such is the case, it follows logically, that, at any moment of time, we all ought to have reached the same level of evolution. But, then, why in fact does inequality exist?[1]

Suppose, on the contrary, that when they incarnate for the first time, the monads are unequal. That inequality can only have two causes: either the animal receptacles differ in the possibilities of evolution which they bring to the incarnate monad, or the monads themselves enjoy unequal capacities to react to impacts of ambient matter. In both cases, we are face to face with a shameful injustice. And who is responsible for it? MAHADEVA, the God of Theosophists. For he it is who produces and outpours the monads on to the mental plane. Why is it that MAHADEVA confers on such and such a monad a higher or lower reactive force? And why does he send such and such a monad into a less good receptacle, less well set up in tools than the one he reserves for another? And as we do not choose the ground of our first incarnation, since, at that moment, the monad is in a state of absolute nakedness, which forbids it all spontaneous act, how could man

---

[1] Theosophists claim to be the champions of absolute justice. Have they thought that just the difference of degree which exists between the positions occupied by the monads on the kosmic planes, already constitutes a flagrant injustice. Why, even temporarily, does an inferior position befall such and such a monad rather than another.

shoulder the responsibility for the consequences which will follow that original inequality ? The real culprit, here, is God, and Theosophists can only blame their God for the so-called reproaches they address to the God of Christians. Certainly, the inequality is perfectly explained. From the moral point of view, the problem remains whole, as it remains if we admit initial inequality.

Let us go farther. Equal or unequal, the human monads, at the moment of their appearance in the Universe, are not amenable to the moral order, since their total nakedness does not allow them to exercise any activity proper to them. They will not be any more amenable to it after their first terrestrial existence. Let us imagine man awakening for the first time to the life of this world. He knows nothing, he has no general directing idea. He expects to learn everything from experience. He is, in short, in the state of those children who learn, by knocking themselves against the walls of their room, to know the sensation of resistance through the pain they feel. And while man, like them, knocks himself against the hard realities of existence, he contracts his first KARMA, that KARMA which, in the course of his existences, will have to be used up to the very end. Now, I ask, can that first KARMA be imputed to him, in justice ? Does it imply the least relation with the moral order ? That " I," that infant-Ego will therefore expiate—for, after all, it is an expiation—acts for which he is not morally to be blamed.

Now, THIS INITIAL KARMA IS THE MODEL, THE PATTERN OF ALL THE KARMAS which accumulate through thousands of existences to come. And why ? Because, from one end of evolution to the other, man, always expecting from experience the impulsive force that must make him progress, will know what he ought to have done only after the achievement of the action. As a scientist, in his laboratory, does not know a phenomenon before having experienced it, so does man know the form of each of his terrestrial existences only after the terrestrial existence is ended. Even the work he does in DEVACHAN does not, strictly speaking, teach him anything about the future, for, if he knows the already lived existences, he knows nothing of the new discoveries which are in store for him. So, he always chases responsibility; he never reaches and never outruns it. And that is the radical vice of all moral theories based on the single criterion of experience. The theory of reincarnation can explain why man suffers from the consequences of his acts. It does not explain why man has deserved his sufferings. Theosophy is a physical doctrine of pain. It is not a moral doctrine.

Shall I add that it is to blame for complicating singularly the problem of suffering itself? What! man, after a terrestrial existence, goes to KAMA-LOKA, and there, as we are taught,[1] he suffers because of the blunders his desire-body committed. Very well. The savage, who committed the fault, a very excusable one, since after all he knows no better, of eating his wife or his old parents, discovers, from the reception given him by his relations, the mistake he has made. Note, by the way, that the said relations are rather hypocritical to act in such a way, as, very likely, they had themselves, in olden times, eaten their fellow-creatures. But, let it be so. The savage, in one way or another, expiates his misconduct. But why, then, when he comes back to earth, will he have to expiate once more the same fault? Why is the suffering of the world beyond increased by the suffering of this world? In the Theosophical doctrine, KAMA-LOKA, and terrestrial KARMA, are a useless repetition. And a theory

[1] *Ancient Wisdom*, Ch. III.

REINCARNATION

which wants to be human owes it to itself, I suppose, to be as sparing of suffering as possible. If not, it creates round destiny an atmosphere of uneasiness, trouble and injustice.

Finally, and this is the third and last grievance I shall bring forward against the doctrine of reincarnation : THE HYPOTHESIS OF SUCCESSIVE LIVES LEGITIMATES, WILLINGLY OR NOT, ALL THE WEAKNESSES OF HUMAN NATURE. Let us see why.

So then the monads follow one another in gradation according to their degree of evolution, on the immensity of the kosmic duration. The virtuous man is an old ego, who has already gone through a numberless cycle of existences. And that is why he is good. The criminal is an infant ego who has hardly started on the way to progress, and that is why he acts badly. Consequence : A criminal, taken before the judges, will listen to the public prosecutor who demands capital punishment for him. The verdict of the jury is certain. The evidence is crushing. Then the accused will stand up, and, looking the judge straight in the eyes, he will say : " Yes, no doubt, I have really committed all the crimes I am accused of. But you have no right to punish me for these crimes. I acted according to my degree of evolution. I am an ' I ' who is beginning. Later on, I shall do better." A murderous people, as represented by its leaders, will be called before the tribunal of nations. That country had dreamt of enslaving the world to its domineering ambitions. Its soldiers shot men, slaughtered women, cut off the hands of little children. Universal indignation falls on these ignoble tormentors. And, there they are, listening to the verdict of the world's conscience which dedicates them to the execration of all civilised persons. Then their voice goes up and protests : " Yes, this is true, we plundered, we killed wantonly. But what did you expect! We are an insufficiently evolved nation, and we have acted within the strict limits of our degree of evolution. Later on we shall do better." And what will the judge, and the members of the tribunal of nations, say, if they profess the Theosophical doctrine? They will remain silent. And they will do well, since, for them, the argument is unanswerable.

Or they will cry, with Mrs. Besant: "Train the criminal and educate him; do not punish him with harshness, for punishment which is revengeful injures still further the Ego who has come into our hands. Certainly do not set him free, no more than you would set free a dangerous animal to prey upon society, for he also is dangerous in his criminal state. But do not make his life miserable. Train him, educate him, and do not let him go until he has shown that he has learnt the lesson of right living."[1]

Educate him! That is easily said. First, it would be necessary to know whether, in the professional criminal, in the leaders of the preying peoples, in a word, in those so-called infant-egos, moral discrimination is so totally absent that the culprit is in no way responsible for his crimes. And, if we want to undertake their education, is it not because we admit the existence of that moral sense which, precisely, makes culprits and criminals? If not, that education is not an education, it is the horrible hulks where men are kicked and made to march under the cudgel.

---

[1] *Popular Lectures*, p. 88. The last sentence of that protestation will certainly give pause to those who know the theosophical doctrine of reincarnation. An INFANT EGO will have to cross many existences before being able to prove, by his conduct, that it is possible for him to live a "right living." It is not only to a temporary prison he ought to be condemned. It is his Ego that ought to be changed for an indefinite number of successive existences. Unhappily, no earthly justice has power to do so.

THEORY OF KNOWLEDGE 197

Educate him! But, with due deference to Mrs. Besant, she herself shows the inanity of the enterprise, from the Theosophical point of view. It is not we who make her say: "You may to some extent mould and modify it, but your powers are very limited. As Ludvig Büchner said, 'Nature is stronger than Nurture.'"[1]

Such is the foundation of Theosophical thought. "Nature is stronger than nurture," because evolution is master of the universe. We have no right to condemn our criminal, because he is irresponsible. We shall in vain attempt to educate him, because "nature is stronger than nurture." So let him go free. And let him be welcome, since, after all, his presence is useful and beneficent. His plunderings will help his neighbours to expiate the consequences of their KARMA.

But I hear the objection: "You Christians take for yourselves the best part," Theosophists will say, "by denouncing the immoral consequences of the doctrine of reincarnation. Begin by making a loyal and salutary examination of conscience. Have we invented the notion of a revengeful and merciless God, who distributes his gifts according to his caprice, and crowns a life of struggles and sacrifices by the tortures of eternal hell? Have we invented that doctrine which appears to us abominable, and which destines the savage, the disinherited child, to misery and crime? Doctor, heal thyself, and thou shalt speak about others."

We could answer, to that direct attack, that the Christian doctrine is not concerned here. Even if we suppose that it is unable to explain the mystery of the present life, does it follow that the Theosophical doctrine is less illogical and more acceptable?

[1] *Popular Lectures*, p. 64.

But, as we are invited to do so, let us say what we Christians think about the justice of God.

We profess, first, that there is a personal God, creator of man and of the Universe, author and keeper of the moral law which, by divine authority, possesses that immutable and absolute value which Theosophy is unable to give it.

We also profess that the inequality of conditions, from a social point of view, is a necessity, but that, from a moral point of view, all men are absolutely equal because they are the children of the same Father. Then we profess that human freedom is not an empty word, and that, in all the force of the term, man is master of his destiny. He can bow before divine law. He can, at will, refuse his adhesion, and, in that case, he is responsible for his refusal.

We also profess that the justice of God does not set itself into motion like a brutal and rigid mechanism. Each will be judged not only according to his doings, but according to the real capacities he has been able to bring to bear to act well. From those who have received much, much will be asked. From those whose effort towards good was paralysed by ignorance, by the influence of surroundings, by evil examples, by hereditary blemishes, God will ask less, because he is a Father and not a tormentor.

We profess, finally, and above all, that divine justice does not express the totality of the Being whom we adore and love with all our hearts. We know that God is infinitely good and that, as soon as there buds in a soul the flower of repentance, which is a fruit of love, the infinite mercy bends over it, and, with a kindly gesture, draws to itself the penitent sinner. Far from feeling an inexorable fatality weighing upon us, we believe that through the apparently absurd drama of life, a work of beauty and of purification is going on, the aim of which is to open the gates of endless happiness to all souls of good will. And, at the same time, we have, of the perfection of our God and of the perfection of Christ, who leads us to Him, such a high and unfathomable idea, that even hundreds of thousands of existences would not be sufficient to bridge, in strict justice, the distance which separates us from Him. We are going to Him, but it is He who walks the greater part of the way. And we are thankful to Him for having given us a single existence of ordeals and struggles in which to utter the simple word with which he deigns to be content : the Yes of our intelligence and the Yes of our heart. As to Hell, we know that therein only fall those who, in the full consciousness of their will, have sinned against light, and have opposed a last and irreparable refusal to the divine entreaties. And, to end, we add that if, amongst Theosophists, there exist souls of good faith, in theory and in practice, those souls, instead of reincarnating to expiate their involuntary error, will go, after their death, to Heaven.

And that is why, we Christians, even apart from the objective reasons which legitimate our choice, prefer Jesus Christ to the MAHATMAS and to Mrs. Annie Besant.

CHAPTER VII

THEOSOPHY AND RELIGIONS

ATTITUDE OF THEOSOPHISTS TOWARDS RELIGION—THEOSOPHY, SOURCE AND TERM OF ALL RELIGIONS—WHY THIS PRETENSION IS NOT JUSTIFIED—AS A MATTER OF FACT, THEOSOPHY IS, PRE-EMINENTLY, THE DESTRUCTIVE AGENT OF ALL RELIGION—WHY IT CANNOT, ITSELF, CLAIM THE TITLE OF RELIGION—THEOSOPHY AND CHRISTIANITY.

THEOSOPHY "is not itself a religion, but it bears to religions the same relation as did the ancient philosophies. It does not contradict them, but explains them. Whatever in any of them is unreasonable, it rejects as necessarily unworthy of the Deity and derogatory to Him; whatever is reasonable in each and all of them it takes up, explains and emphasizes, and thus combines all into one harmonious whole."[1] These lines of Mr. Leadbeater define, roughly speaking, the attitude that Theosophists pretend to observe towards religion in general and historical religions. Is this attitude legitimate? We intend to answer this question in the present study.

* * *

In the main, Theosophy assumes the position of judge of all cults, and, moreover, of all philosophies, as a moment ago it took up the position of judge of Science and of scientific hypothesis. These haughty manners can no longer astonish us, now that we have penetrated the spirit and made clear the broad lines of the secret doctrine.

[1] Leadbeater, *An Outline of Theosophy*, p. 4.

THEOSOPHY AND RELIGIONS

There is, at first, that visible and tangible fact that the present humanity is divided, in the matter of religion, into a quantity of sects, confessions and churches. Such a diversity has, without doubt, real and deep causes. If we look more closely, we realise that all those religions are of very unequal value. The distance is great, from the coarse fetishism of the savage to the monotheism of the prophets of Israel. For the Theosophist, religious differences constitute a new confirmation, brought by experience, of the principles which are dear to him ; man is diverse religiously as he is socially, because he evolves, because he reincarnates : " Circumstances make peoples adopt the religion which corresponds to their degree of evolution, but every religious cult answers only to a particular stage of their life."[1] On the way to progress, religions follow each other in gradation, and each of them has only a transitory value. No belief, no dogmatic formula, no cult, no practice, is equal to truth, to absolutism. Religion changes, evolves, with the men who profess it.

Shall we conclude, thence, that Religion, with its moving and fleeting face, is only a tissue of illusions and errors ? Theosophists do not mean it so. Just as, in the soul of the savage, the soul of the future " Thinker " outlines itself, so the lowest and most shapeless religions contain the promise of the highest and the most perfect ones.

But a difficulty appears. Everybody can see the multiplicity of religious groupings. But, as soon as it comes to pronouncing about them a judgment of value, the necessity of discovering an infallible criterion is imposed. Monotheism is superior to fetishism. Why ? Because, in our opinion, the idea of one God represents a conquest, a progress of the human mind. The Theosophist himself

[1] *Evoluisme*, p. 222.

possesses his criterion, which he asks neither from traditional philosophy, nor, still less, from Christian revelation. His criterion is occult science. A religion will therefore be all the more perfect that is nearer, by its beliefs, to the pure doctrines of Theosophy, to that divine Wisdom, the authenticity of which is guaranteed by the uninterrupted testimony of the MAHATMAS.

We know the fundamental articles of the Theosophical CREDO : God, universal soul of the world, present in everything ; progressive evolution of human soul into super-human soul, and, later on, into divine soul, by reincarnation and ascension on to the "formless" planes. Let us add three articles which are the development and the consequence of the first ones : the Trinity or Trimûrti ; the Hierarchy of divine Beings, agents of the laws of the Universe, and, finally, the human Fraternity. With this septenary, we have the total of the truths which, in the eyes of the adepts of occultism, allow discernment and appreciation of the perfection of a historical or living religion.

That is not all. When Theosophy assumes the right of distributing highest honours to religions, not only does it assume the functions of a judge, but it acts as an owner. It takes back a property which belongs to it, because, as a matter of fact, " all religions are the branches of the same trunk which is called Theosophy, or ancient wisdom."[1]

Ancient Wisdom " was taught to all people." At what time ? When men " were provided with the cerebro-spinal system, and, consequently, with intelligence and reason. In these remote times appeared Great Divine Beings who belonged to a previous humanity (THE BIBLE CALLS THEM THE SONS OF GOD). They guided and taught the human race as chiefs, kings, and priests. They

[1] *Leçons*, p. 15.

THEOSOPHY AND RELIGIONS

founded in the ancient Lemuria a brilliant civilisation, of which famous traces are to be found in Easter Island. (See " La Doctrine Secrète et Pierre Loti.")[1]

But how is it that ancient wisdom has, through the ages, degenerated and taken the forms of those religions, none of which reproduces, in all its primitive purity, the primeval doctrine ? The answer is rather complex, but how suggestive ! In principle, it would be inaccurate to pronounce the word " degeneracy." The teaching delivered at the dawn of ages by the Great Divine Beings, was gathered and kept " by the members of the Great occult Hierarchy." These " are human beings who have completed their evolution, and who guide the evolution of the whole Race." And they are precisely the ones who " have founded the different religions."[2] But, instead of revealing all that teaching, of which he is the guardian, each new founder " chooses one of the great Truths of divine Wisdom in order to build the basis of a new Religion, appropriate to the needs, to the degree of civilisation, to the degree of evolution, to the climatic conditions of the peoples or of the races which he is addressing. This fact always happens at the advent of a new race or sub-race,[3] which is, in this way, endowed with a new civilisation."[4] The partial and fragmentary character presented by each religion taken apart involves no peril, as long as members of the Great Occult Hierarchy are present to confront the portion of faith vulgarised by religion, with the complete whole which is the source of it. And here intervenes the famous distinction between

[1] Ibid. p. 14.
[2] The novel, issued from the powerful imagination of M. Edouard Schuré, and which is entitled *Les Grands Initiés* is only the development of that Theosophical idea.
[3] About races and sub-races, see above, Ch. III.
[4] This quotation and the preceding ones are taken from *Leçons*, p. 15.

esoteric and exoteric teaching, this one " outer and public," that one " confined to a small number, to those who are worthy of it."[1] Religious decadence appears when, as a consequence of the authoritative blindness of the visible leaders of the churches, the esoteric teaching is put aside. The result of this disjunction, of this divorce, is fatal: the religions have lost the true and deep meaning of their beliefs or of their rites; they fall into a narrow formalism, they become motionless and crush the masses under their unbearable yoke. We shall see in a moment for whom those reproaches are meant.

But if we grant to Theosophists the privilege of possessing, in its unalterable integrity, the " treasure of esoteric truth," we shall understand how the adepts in ancient wisdom cannot be content to form a platonic judgment on such and such a religious form. They owe to themselves and to the doctrine of which they are the happy owners to interfere actively in the religious life of peoples, to set errors right again, and to give back the breath of life to dead or dying organisms. From that standpoint, their programme is condensed in a very simple formula: little by little, to re-introduce esoterism in the religions which have forgotten or misunderstood it. And their apostolic zeal will be all the more attentive and keen according as the religion in question is more remote from the esoteric doctrine.

That commentary renders more precise the sense of Mr. Leadbeater's text, quoted at the beginning of the present chapter. Theosophists—we chiefly mean the leaders of the sect—bear, on their predestined foreheads, the seal of great religious reformers. And, once more, the question is asked: Have they the right to take that title, and to attribute to themselves that mission?

* * *

[1] Ibid. p. 15.

THEOSOPHY AND RELIGIONS 205

At first, and as an introduction, let us note the strange *petitio principii* which hovers, menacingly, over the origins of the Secret Doctrine itself. To be sure, the explanation given by Theosophists, of the diversity of beliefs and cults, offers all the appearances of logic. Humanity evolves. Therefore Religion evolves with it. Religious truth, as well as philosophical or scientifical truth, is going forward. It is becoming, it is making itself. It can be found at the termination, and not at the starting point of evolution.

Now, all at once, there springs up, at the beginning of the ascending movement, a complete, achieved, definitive doctrine, which is going to be the first and only source of all the future religions. We should very much like to know whence comes that magnificent improvisation. It is introduced to us as an inheritance from the Great Divine Beings. Those Great Beings are, in reality, we have been told, " men who belonged to a previous humanity." Let us be logical. If all, in the Theosophical system is ruled by the scheme of a rigorous evolutionism, we are bound to imagine older humanity as inferior in every respect to the humanities which have come after. Such is evolutive logic. Let us drive it forward to its conclusion, and suppose that those so-called Divine Beings, who are, really, only men, have belonged to a kosmic manifestation prior to the one to which our oldest ancestors belong as we do. A legitimate hypothesis, for, as we know, the Universe passes through periods of rest, during which it is completely indrawn, with ISHVARA, into the bosom of the Great All. But we know, too, that each new manifestation marks a progress on the previous one, and begins the ascension at the point where it had been left. Thus, whatever be their origin, the famous divine Beings we are speaking of are less evolved than the primitive races of which they were the teachers. That primitive race, we are told, is really called the Lemurian race. Here it is, exactly described by the pen of a Theosophist who publishes his works at the Headquarters of the French Theosophical Society: "The men of this race had gigantic and powerful bodies; had they not got to struggle against animals of prodigious size and strength? Our sharp weapons could not have cut their skin. To hearing and touching, sight was added; first, a single eye in the middle of the forehead (cyclops), then two symmetrical eyes. The monosyllabic language appeared; intelligence developed its rudiments when was formed, very slowly, the cerebro-spinal system, together with the brain."[1] They have as descendants "the natives of Australia, of Tasmania, whose bodies are hairy, and the last specimen of which will soon have disappeared. Most of the negro races derive from them as well."[3] Such were the first pupils to receive the sublime teachings of Ancient Wisdom. And we wonder how such men, whose intelligence was rudimentary, who spoke a monosyllabic language, and who, as a crowning happiness, lacked the sense of hearing,[2] were able to climb the abstruse slopes of Theosophy. The question is useless, since their divine instructors, issued from a much older evolutive stage, must have reached, according to the very principles of the doctrine, a still lower degree on the ladder of progress. Theosophy ruthlessly gives itself the lie, by putting, at the beginning of evolution, a teaching, a doctrinal body which can only be the fruit of the ascensional progress of humanity. And, if such is the case, what becomes of the claim, put forward by Theosophists, to possess the initial source wherefrom have come the historical religions? The claim is contrary to the

[1] *Leçons*, p. 138.
[2] The sense of hearing appears only with the fourth race, called the Atlantean race.

THEOSOPHY AND RELIGIONS

most essential data of the system. Theosophy cannot be a source. It could, at the utmost, be a resultant.

And if it is a resultant, what right have its adepts to wish to impose it on us as a definitive and final solution of all the problems which haunt the human mind ? To proclaim oneself as having found " the absolute truth concerning spiritual things,"[1] and afterwards to establish that title of exclusive property on the study of the marvels which are made in that immense laboratory of the Kosmos, where particular forces are ceaselessly at work to make the globes and the humanities evolve : these two affirmations are contradictory. Human intelligence, philosophically speaking, holds as true what does not change. A principle is true when it realises the conditions which make it immutable in the past, in the present, in the future, for eternity. But to subordinate the notion of Truth to the events which happen in the immense laboratory of the Kosmos, is to kill the notion of Truth, for the Kosmos itself is the theatre of an eternal evolution. And once more, even on this last point, Theosophists could not, without going farther than their means, promise to us that the " marvels " of the future will be the same as the " marvels " of yesterday and of to-day. Who can know the surprises that the One Existence, " unreachable and incognisable " reserves for the observers of the future ? If that Existence is unreachable, his designs are impenetrable. How do Theosophists know them ? How do they know that the next manifestation of the Great All will be accomplished on a plane similar to the one which, according to them, presides over the manifestation in which we are actors and spectators ? Do they not need some audacity to impose, so to speak, on the infinite richness of the universal soul, only one way of expressing itself ? And who knows whether the universal soul of

[1] *Esoteric Buddhism*, p. 13.

the world has no other resources—if it means to manifest itself—than to use the evolutive process? Is not the breath of BRAHMA powerful enough to emit in one blast what he outbreathes, actually, with an incalculable slowness? And who, finally, can know whether, one day, at his pleasure, BRAHMA will not keep in for ever that breath that causes the world to exist? Theosophy, except by disowning itself, has no right to tear before our eyes the veil which hides that formidable unknown. It can be the science of one moment, of a stage in the history of worlds. It is certainly not the science of which we can say that by it we look right into the abyss of eternal and absolute truth. What is true, at the stage we have reached, will probably have ceased to be so at the next stage, either because the Universe will have gone on evolving, or because it will evolve no more, and more so, of course, if it has gone back for ever into the "Super-Consciousness" of the incognizable Being. The pretension of Theosophists to assume the rôle of doctors of truth solves itself, finally, in an acknowledgment of abysmal ignorance. And that ignorance concerns principally what causes the religious souls of all ages to thrill: the ultimate "Why?" of human destiny. One has no right to take the direction of the intellectual and religious movement in humanity, when, to the gravest and most anxious questions, one has only to answer: truth, like God, is not, it is being made. We shall know it when the eternal making of things, in which we believe with all our souls, will be ended. But as it is part of the nature of an eternal making, never to end, we shall never know. And one has still less right to assume the mission of correcting, redressing and enlightening the beliefs or the systems, when the doctrine from which one takes one's inspiration is false. Above Theosophy there is reason. And, in the eye of reason, Theosophical pantheism is

THEOSOPHY AND RELIGIONS

an error; Theosophical evolution is an error; Theosophical reincarnation is an error. Even if all the historical religions—and it would be a difficult task, for an impartial historian, to prove it—had, under the exoteric or the esoteric form, professed the fundamental dogmas of occult science, it would not follow at all that the latter would have the right of crystallizing the whole of humanity round a doctrine that sound reason could not possibly assimilate. A systematised error is more dangerous than a spontaneous one. But when one and the other join hands, humanity walks rapidly on the road to illusion.

Such are the real titles, that Theosophy can claim to serve as a guide to the religious thought of our time. They are not of those which impose themselves by their indisputable value. That can be proved, if necessary, in a still more precise way.

* * *

Without lingering longer to discuss the origins and the extent of the secret doctrine, one consequence of the above considerations stands out clearly: Theosophy is the goal towards which walk, by a sort of infallible and unavoidable attraction, all the religions of the world. In other words, the particular religions constitute only steps, stages on an ascending road, at the end of which Theosophy alone subsists. As the authors of a great Theosophical treatise say very well: " On the superior plane of thoughts, where man comes nearer to God by his progress towards the one truth, divergencies between the three roads which lead to it—Science, Religion, Philosophy, WEAKEN PROGRESSIVELY. In their evolution, the three of them, like the radii of a circle, converge towards the same central point—truth. The ultimate truth being one, according as the different religions, sciences or philosophies climb towards it, the differences between them disappear, and they come nearer to one another."[1] Let us carry that reconciliation to its limit: differences have completely disappeared, and the occult science, expression of the One Truth, remains the only master of the human thought.

We cannot insist too much on that generally little known aspect of Theosophical teaching. When Mr. Leadbeater tells us that Theosophy does not "contradict" religions but "explains" them, he only half-expresses, he only intimates, the deep idea of the system. He gives to understand, and those who are kindred with him are inexhaustible on the same subject—that Theosophical faith can perfectly well accommodate itself to all the religious CREDOS. That accommodation—we shall see whether it is possible—represents only, if I may say so, the static point of view of occult doctrine. Religions exist in fact. Their existence must therefore be tolerated, for, to tell the truth, they do not seem ready to resorb themselves into the "higher" thought of which they are supposed to be the fragmentary and more or less disfigured expression. But if we consider things from the dynamic point of view, which is, after all, the point of view of evolution, and, consequently, the true Theosophical point of view, everything changes, and we are obliged to conceive Theosophy as the centre, the focus, the fold which particular religions must reach, sooner or later, and where they will be blended together.

This being laid down, we are allowed to conclude that Theosophy appears to us as being, pre-eminently, the destructive agent of all religion. And why? Well, the reason is obvious. It is given to us, and this time without any reticence, by Mr. Leadbeater: "Theosophy is not itself a religion." If, on the one hand, all

[1] *Evoluisme*, p. 229-230.

THEOSOPHY AND RELIGIONS

religions tend to blend with that higher doctrine called Theosophy, and if, on the other hand, Theosophy is not a religion : then at the limit, that is, at the precise moment when fusion is realised, Religion has disappeared. And by what will it be replaced ? By a doctrine, by a Science.

The incomprehension of human nature could not be pushed further. Theosophists fail here by an extraordinary ignorance of psychology ; this ignorance reassures us fully, moreover, as to the future of an attempt doomed, beforehand, to miscarriage. It could have some chance of success, if the religious feelings consisted only and exactly of an intellectual need, of a desire for knowledge. And, certainly, we shall not be the ones to deny that there is an intellectual element in Religion. The best feelings deviate and go astray if they do not blossom in the pure atmosphere of truth. The monstrous excesses into which some ancient religions have fallen prove it abundantly. But there is, in religion, something more than the desire to know. There is a feeling of dependence on those mysterious and powerful beings who are called Gods, which implies respect, fear, sometimes also love. There are, to express this feeling, ritual gestures, sacrifices, prayers, a cult. And moral life is impregnated, in its turn, and coloured, with that same feeling which leads conscience and inspires fidelity to duty. Such are the integral contents of religion. And such is what Theosophists want to replace, sooner or later, by a dry intellectualism. Between Religion and Theosophy, there is a gulf that has never been and will never be bridged.

I want no other testimony of it than that unbelievable fiction to which Theosophists are obliged to resort to explain the origin and the diversities of religions. What ? There were, at the beginning of the present humanity, illuminated, initiated beings who were in possession of all the secrets of divine science. Those great masters were, moreover, revered chiefs, venerated by the peoples. How is it that those famous doctors have been neither understood nor obeyed? We are told that, then, humanity was not able to grasp the sublimity of occult teachings. We willingly believe it. In such a case, they ought to have kept silent, for we can apply to their conduct the rather unkind remark suggested to a convinced Theosophist by the magnificent spectacle of Christian apostleship: " To want to bring savages to Christianity, as do some fanatical missionaries, is an evolutionist error."[1] Let us transpose, and say with Theosophists conscious of their principles: " To want to bring savages of the Lemurian race, who hardly possessed a rudiment of intelligence, to profess the dogmas of occult science, as did some fanatical Great Masters, was an evolutionist error." Yes, the Great Masters would have been wiser to keep silent. They did not. But, as they were clever people, they have extinguished the splendour of occult doctrines, which nobody wanted, and they have resorted to an expedient. And what is that expedient? The foundations of religions. A strange solution, if ever there was one! For after all it is evident that the immense majority of historical religions profess beliefs which have nothing in common with Theosophical ideas. Let us not speak here of esoterism, which, according to Theosophists themselves, has always been the jealously guarded privilege of very rare Initiates. The religious mass has not known and does not know the ideas of Mrs. Besant. There are in the world only two doctrines of which the formula comes near Theosophy: Brahmanism and Buddhism, to which, precisely, some historians deny the title of religion. Yet, in India,

[1] *Evoluisme*, p. 96.

Brahmanism has been blended with the popular beliefs, to constitute Hinduism, which is evidently not pure Brahmanism. As to Buddhism, everybody knows that the religious instinct has taken a rapid revenge on the practical atheism of its founder. Buddha had put God aside: men avenged themselves by making him a god. In short, historical reality superabundantly proves it: even from the point of view of " belief," that is from the doctrinal and intellectual point of view, religion, through history, does not show a Theosophical character: there is, already, on that side, a difference, a considerable divergence. And to whom must we attribute this divergence? To Theosophists themselves. They have, from the beginning, and in the person of their Great Masters, played the equivocal part which consists in keeping for oneself the integral truth, and leaving the rest of the world to flounder and to sink in the deep ruts of error. All the religions that are not pantheistic and that admit personal gods, distinct from Universe; all the religions that ignore the benefits of the kosmic evolution and do not want to hear about SAMSARA, the fatal wheel of indefinite reincarnations; all the religions that refuse to conceive the complete identity of man with God: all those religions, I say, are, theosophically, in error. And to whom are the errors to be imputed? To the founders of religions. And who are those founders? Initiates, i.e., Theosophists.

Once more, there is here an improbable fiction. But that fiction betrays a deep truth. Do you want to know why, from the beginning, the Great Masters, if we suppose that they have existed, have been obliged to compound with Religion? It is because, even at that time, Religion was a human fact, with which they had to reckon. And for good reasons it is not the Great Masters who have invented Religion. It is Religion which has always put up, by instinct, an insurmountable wall against all attempts to volatilize it into pure intellectualism, be it true or false. And as, in India, the religious instinct has reacted against Brahmanism by kneeling at the feet of Civa, of Vishnu, even at the feet of Alcyone ; as the religious instinct of all the peoples of the far East—Chinese, Corean, Indo-Chinese—has reacted against Buddhism by deifying Buddha, Amitaba, Avolokiteçvara, and all the multitude of the Bodhisattva, so, to-day as well as yesterday, to-morrow as well as to-day, religious humanity does and will react against those doctrinarians who, under the pretext of enlightening the letter and the rites, kill the spirit of religion. For, what religious humanity desires is not only to know, but to adore, to serve, and, if possible, to love the object of its adoration and of its sacrifices. Theosophy, which, by the place it assigns itself in human evolution, means to resorb in itself, sooner or later, the positive religions, comes into contact with a force which outdoes it. And it will break against that force. To its entreaties, the truly religious souls, clearly divining the goal they would be led to, will always be able to answer, when necessary, by applying to whom it may concern, the verse of a personage of tragedy : " I embrace my rival, but it is to choke him."[1]

* * *

It is true that, sometimes, Theosophy seems to give the illusion of gratifying the religious need. It is not " itself a religion," and yet to be a little so suits it rather well : does it not profess that there exists a whole hierarchy of superior beings without whose help man cannot climb up the steep path of evolution ? With what piety, with what eloquence, does Mrs. Besant often describe the beneficent action of those Devas, of those Gods, whose

[1] Racine, *Britannicus*.

function is to "guide evolution according to the design of Ishvara!"[1] And what impressive eloquence is in these words: "Step by step we have to climb from the manifested to the unmanifested, and in His compassionate love, God veils Himself in forms of beauty to attract the human heart, in order that the human heart may rise adoringly to His feet, and that some portion of His life, pouring down thereinto, may enable the Self of the worshipper to realise even partially its unity with Him."[2] Now, without the Devas "these wills of ours would work infinite confusion, and the world would never complete its evolution, would never roll upwards to its place at the feet of God."[3] So that the concord of human wills is realised by the DEVAS, who, "mould the forms in which the growing life is to express itself."[4] And when form becomes an obstacle to progress, they break it, even if they be obliged, in the interest of human beings, to use violence, and to let loose one of those terrible catastrophes which deliver souls from the bondage of matter, circumstances, social surroundings. In short, it is they who preside over the KARMA of nations and regulate the conditions of the punishment in store for the peoples who have prevaricated against justice.[5]

It is probable that Mr. Leadbeater has read those lines in the works from the President of the Theosophical Society. We, the profane, may wonder whether the eyes of Mrs. Besant's fellow-worker did not grow dim when reading again the sentence I have already quoted several times: "Theosophy is not itself a religion." It is indeed a religion, since it tells us about protecting DEVAS, and, moreover, about that "worship" which makes the

[1] *Evolution*, p. 54.
[2] *Evolution*, p. 54.
[3] *Evolution*, p. 58.
[4] *Evolution*, p. 58.
[5] *Evolution*, 3rd Lecture, Passim.

human heart "rise adoringly" up to the feet of God!
Who is right, Mr. Leadbeater or Mrs. Besant? It is true
that, in the book from which I borrow these quotations,
Mrs. Besant addresses a Hindu audience, and that, considering that circumstance, the esoteric teaching had to
be adapted to the readily polytheist mentality of the
hearers. But the question is not solved by this remark.
For, in the majority of the books by the famous President,
we see again God and the Devas.

Is Theosophy a religion, or is it not?
In order to solve that delicate question, let us put aside
all the accidental considerations that can be or are dictated by the necessities of propaganda. It is clear,
indeed, that, religions being not yet ripe—we know why—
for the blending of their doctrines with the occult one, it
is mightily important to be careful about transitions.
To interpret common beliefs in a Theosophical sense,
would be already a progress. That progress could only
be reached if Theosophists resign themselves to speaking
the ordinary language. To Hindus, Hindu language will
be spoken. To Christians, Christian language. And as,
after all, all the books and all the lectures published by the
THEOSOPHICAL SOCIETY are subordinate to an aim of
propaganda, we must use them with precaution. It is
not from an outer garment of Theosophical thought that
we must ask enlightenment. It is to the thought itself,
to the essential principles of the doctrine, that we must,
before everything, come back.

Now, if we place ourselves on this strong ground, the
solution cannot be doubtful. The question, in sooth,
comes back to these clear and unequivocal terms: can an
evolutionist and pantheistic system claim the right
to be a religion? Is there room in this system for a God
that we can adore, and for beings radically higher than

THEOSOPHY AND RELIGION

humanity, who can be surrounded with a cult of respect and veneration ? And I dare to answer plainly : no, there is not.

What then is this God towards whom could ascend the Theosophical adoration ? Is it the "Super-Consciousness," the " One Being, without a second " ? This anonymous God, this " unreachable and incognisable " God is separated from us by a bottomless gulf. This God ignores us, for, being the Super-Conciousness, he cannot know the whirlpools, issued from his eternal substance, in the depths of which we are carried along and rolled like so many straws. He ignores us, we ignore him. There is no possible relation with Him.

Is this God the great solar Logos, the Centre of Consciousness of our Universe, who expands in the triplicity of his kosmic functions ? Nobody will ever believe that this narrow and limited God, brought back to the proportions of a mere planetary demiurge, can have any right to the adoration of anybody. God, for us, is the Infinite, or he is not. Moreover, and this criticism embraces at once ISHVARA and the multitude of the Devas he employs in his service, who are they exactly, these high, or supposed to be high, beings, who are offered to us as objects of religious feelings ? What is the distance between them and us ? The mere distance of a degree of evolution : " Men are Gods in the making, and we are preparing to discharge the functions of the Gods."[1]

Precious words, confession which enlightens all and dispenses us from going farther. While the Super-Consciousness sinks into the retreat of its impenetrable solitude, the rest of the divine beings come so near to us that really they are identical with us in essence, in nature, and, in different degrees, in powers. They are supermen. And it would be vain to try and establish an ex-

[1] *Evolution*, p. 89.

ception in favour of ISHVARA. ISHVARA, the great Logos, being, by definition, the fruitage of an evolved Universe, totalises, in his transient consciousness, all the humanity evolved in the course of a kosmic manifestation. He is humanity itself, blended in the identity of a personality one and gigantic.

And we have there, let us note it on our way, the secret of that universal fraternity which, as we said a moment ago, is one of the articles of the Theosophical CREDO. " The consciousness of this inner unity, the recognition of the One Self dwelling equally in all, is the one sure foundation of brotherhood ; all else save this is frangible."[1] We are brothers, because, profoundly, a substantially identical soul vibrates in us, but a soul which manifests itself by the infinite diversity of the degrees of evolution : " Identity of essential life, and differences in the stages reached in the manifestation of that life."[2] And, indeed, what reason should I have to hate my brother, when my brother is I at another degree of evolution ? But the reasoning could be pushed in another direction. What reason should I have to adore any deva, when that deva is I, at a higher degree of evolution ? And what reason should I have to adore ISHVARA, since ISHVARA is, once more, I, to that supreme degree of evolution where the whole Universe solves itself in the Unity of universal consciousness ?

And if we desire, at all costs, to grant Theosophy the name of a religion, we shall be obliged to say that Theosophy is THE RELIGION OF HUMANITY, that is, a religion where man is, at the same time, the worshipper and the object of adoration. The deification of man, such is the basis of Theosophy. But one will agree, we cannot use here the word religion without subjecting the word to a

[1] *Ancient Wisdom*, p. 172. [2] *Ancient Wisdom*, p. 173.

THEOSOPHY AND RELIGIONS

regrettable twist. For, in all times, and in all places, humanity, at all stages, at all levels of civilization, has understood that, to make a religion, it is necessary to have at least two—man and God. If God and man are identical, religion has no more *raison d'être*. It goes back to nothingness.

Who is right, Mr. Leadbeater or Mrs. Annie Besant? It is Mr. Leadbeater : " Theosophy is not itself a religion." But we are allowed to think that, on this point, Mrs. Annie Besant shares the opinion of her fellow-worker

* * *

We could end, with those lines, the study of the relations of Theosophy to religion. However, we shall be allowed to add a few words on the special relations of Theosophy to the Christian religion, and chiefly to Catholicism.

Badly informed minds could wonder about the hostility, imperfectly hidden under the veil of current formulas, that Theosophists cherish towards Catholic Christianity. While the other religions enjoy an almost shadowless benevolence, Catholicism hears itself being told, amongst praises which are not really meant for it, hard words, devoid of all spirit of fraternity : " Love one another," Christ has said, so justifying the name of Lord of Love that is given to him in India. " Accept suffering according to my example " could be the second formula of his teaching. TO KNOW HOW TO LOVE AND TO SUFFER, such are the two poles of Christian religion. The essence of Christianity consists in the idea that every man must aspire to the perfection of Christ. How to reach it Christ shows us by his teachings, by his life and by his passion."[1] This is the praise. It is equivocal, for Christians have never, after all, believed that Jesus Christ was an avatar of Vishnu, or that their religion does

[1] *Evoluisme*, p. 99-100.

not include any other teachings than those of charity and suffering. Let us pass on. " The light shed by Christ in the West has been of an extraordinary splendour, and if the Christian religion built up during the first three centuries of our era had kept the teaching of primitive Christianity, it could have become the most beautiful of all . . . . Unfortunately the iniquities of the Inquisition, the excesses which brought on the Reformation, the exclusiveness, the intransigence, the clericalism, and finally, the abandonment of the great ideas of the high intellectual and moral culture of the Fathers of the Church, to sink into a ritualism which absorbs all the religious spirit and no longer gives satisfaction to present humanity, at least amongst us—have considerably tarnished its lustre . . . . France, at the present moment, needs another religion, in accordance with her degree of evolution ; let us hope, for her sake, that it will not be long in appearing."[1] This is the blame, and we must acknowledge, with all convenient humility, that it is much franker than the praise.

We shall not be expected to refute, here, the dark allegations that Theosophy bears against Catholicism. The " iniquities " of the Inquisition are of an age somewhat posterior to the third century. The abuses that brought on the Reformation had not prevented the Catholic religion from giving a splendid inspiration to the Christian life of the seventeenth century—see Saint Francois de Sales and Saint Vincent de Paul—and this time coincides precisely with a revival of the patristic studies—see the works of the Jesuit Petau and the Benedictine editions. Exclusiveness and intransigence are words the sense of which depends principally on the standpoint wherefrom they are defined. Clericalism is a rather old and hypocritical epithet, the exact signification of which Gambetta himself would have

[1] *Evoluisme*, p. 100.

THEOSOPHY AND RELIGIONS

been much put to, to give. As to " ritualism," its responsible authors are, as it seems, those superficial Christians who have never taken the pains to search into their religion, and who transform faith and religious practices into a sort of article of the mundane code. But, as a matter of fact, has Theosophy nothing to do with fashion and snobbishness?

Those reproaches put aside, there remain two fundamental objections: Christianity, in Catholicism, has swerved from its primitive orientation, and, moreover, the law of evolution claims, at the present moment, another religion.

This last affirmation[1] gives us the key to the problem

---

[1] The first is based on such fanciful commentaries on the Scriptures and on the patristic texts that it would really be too much of an honour for Theosophists if we took the pains to redress it. It is sufficient to denounce the tendency which inspires all that ridiculous and wily exegesis. It is a question of " re-introducing," at all costs, in Catholicism, that famous esoterism which is at the source and at the basis of all religions. We know what is to be thought of this fiction (see above). But, to " re-introduce " esoterism, it is necessary for it to have existed at the origin of Christianism. Therefore there will be an esoteric Christianism. Jesus has taught two doctrines, one for the crowd, the other for the " initiates." After this, Theosophists try their best to reconstruct that esoterism, which, of course, must coincide with that of pagan religions. Then comes a fruitless search through texts, a gibberish of mutilated quotations, twisted from their obvious sense, a display of erudition which, to prove something, lacks only loyalty and common sense. We firmly refuse to follow Theosophists on that ground. It is losing time to force open doors, by demonstrating, for instance, that the TRIMURTI has nothing in common with the " Trinity " (where have the adepts in occult science learnt that Word=love and Spirit=intelligence ?), or that reincarnation is not implied in these two texts : " Elijah is come already (St. Matt. xvii. 12) and " He that overcometh, I will make him a pillar in the temple of my God, and he shall go out thence no more " (Revel. iii. 12), or that, finally, Mr. Schuré, in his *Grands Initiés* scoffs at history as Mrs. A. Besant scoffs at logic.

we want to solve. Between Catholicism and Theosophy, there is no possible understanding, because, at the present moment, Catholicism is the only religion which unequivocally refuses to enter into the way of evolution. Now, after the principles of occult science, each religion " adapts itself to a definite humanity. It ceases to answer its needs if it does not know how to follow evolution. That is why a religion which does not evolve is a religion which is dying."[1] The Catholics who flatter themselves on reconciling their Christian CREDO with the Theosophical doctrines will be wise to meditate on the meaning of those words. We can only be Theosophists on the condition of disowning the dogmas of the Church, in the sense that the Church gives them.

Thus, then, Catholicism does not evolve, from the doctrinal point of view. And, consequently, it cannot be in harmony with a system of which evolution is, so to speak, the soul and life. That doctrinal immobility, as we readily admit, is a fact.

But any fact asks for an explanation. Why does the Catholic Church refuse to evolve? It can only be for one or the other of the following reasons: either it is behind the times, or it possesses truth. If it is behind the times, why do Theosophists take such pains to fight it? According to the principles of the evolutive doctrine, they must think that Catholicism answers a present need of souls on their way to progress. Why do they not let the Church die a natural death? It would be rather cruel of them to deprive the human monads of a help which is needed by some to progress. Or else Catholicism possesses, or thinks it possesses, truth. Now, I do not think there is, in the world, a single doctrinal power that dares publish such a claim, not even Theosophy, which, if

[1] *Evoluisme*, p. 222.

THEOSOPHY AND RELIGIONS

t is consistent with itself, must repeat, with a certain Roman procurator: " QUID EST VERITAS ? " What is truth ? Such a claim deserves to be examined. Let Theosophists put themselves, with all their freedom of mind, under the schooling of our doctors, of our theologians, of our apologists. We are at their disposal. And if we do not manage to convince them, let them be reassured, we shall not burn them.

That objective attitude, the only one we ask from them, will save them the trouble they take to invent, in its entirety, a romance of the Christian origins, which nobody, if he is well informed, has ever credited. Christ avatar of Vishnu, esoteric Christianity, the dogma of reincarnation preached by the evangelists and the Fathers of the Church, even that unhappy man, blind from birth, made use of in order to throw dust in the eyes of ignorant and naïve Christians :[1] nothing of all this will ever replace

---

[1] See St. John ix, 1-3. This text has gained such a celebrity amongst Theosophists, that we make in its favour an exception to the above-given rule. Here is the commentary of Mrs. Besant : " So again we find the disciples taking reincarnation for granted in asking whether blindness from birth was a punishment for a man's sins, and Jesus in answer not rejecting the possibility of ante-natal sin, but only excluding it as causing the blindness in the special instance " (*Ancient Wisdom*, p. 28). The first part of the explanation bears discussion. It is possible that the apostles have made themselves the echo of a popular belief in the coming back of the souls of the dead into the bodies of the living. As to the second part, which aims at defining Christ's innermost thought, it is inadmissible.

[1*] Theosophists admit that, in his answer, Jesus does not speak either for or against reincarnation. Therefore, from a strictly logical point of view, the alleged text proves nothing.

[2*] It is asserted that, if Christ had not approved of the doctrine of reincarnation, he would have protested against the belief to which the apostles seemed to allude. Therefore, that doctrine is implicitly admitted by him. Really, Christ goes to the very heart of the problem. If, in his innermost thought, he had approved the doctrine of KARMA—no other is in question, as a matter of fact—he

that very simple work which would consist in confronting the humblest of our catechisms with the letter and the spirit of our Gospels.

As you see, we do not want to take tragically the antagonism which Theosophists establish between them and ourselves. Doctrinal antagonism: it exists. It is and will remain irreducible. To become a Theosophist, one must be an apostate. Antagonism of persons: it does not exist. The born Catholics will always be happy to explain to Theosophists why they can be neither pantheists, nor materialists, nor believers in reincarnation.

And if the day were to come when Theosophy, helped by some very occult power, in the name of that fraternity which has its rather narrow source in ISHVARA'S heart, would wish to force true Catholics to choose between the One Existence and the God we adore, the true Catholics would probably be content to repeat, with Father Captier and the victims of the Commune: " En avant ! pour le Bon Dieu ! "

would have rejected, as a dangerous error, the possibility of an external intervention being opposed to the inflexible working of the laws of immanent justice. If God possesses the supreme control of human fate, if He can cure physical infirmities (as He cures the moral ones), it proves that the theory of Karma is false.

3*The words and acts of Christ usually have a general value and import ; that conclusion results of the study of the Gospels (see, for instance, the episodes of the fruitless fig-tree, of the woman taken in adultery, etc.). Through the case of the man blind from birth, Jesus expresses a principle : " Neither did the man sin, nor his parents," which implies the repudiation of the *theories* of which the disciples make a particular application.

CHAPTER VIII

THEORY OF KNOWLEDGE

PECULIAR CHARACTER OF THEOSOPHICAL " KNOWLEDGE "—THE TWO STAGES OF " KNOWLEDGE "—KNOWLEDGE " BY IMAGES "—THE ILLUSION—THE POWER OF THOUGHT—HOW THE ADEPT ESCAPES DANGER—" INTUITIVE " KNOWLEDGE ; ITS TERM ; THE INNER VISION OF THE UNIVERSAL SELF—THE LAST WORD OF HUMAN DESTINY, ACCORDING TO THEOSOPHY—CONCLUSION.

EVERY philosophical system contains a theory of knowledge, that is, a certain way of conceiving the relations between the human intelligence and reality. The attitude taken by the thinker towards that primordial problem is reverberated through the whole doctrine. The diversity of conclusions, in metaphysics as in morals, is due, first of all, to the difference of principles which define the notion of truth and the means to reach it. Theosophy does not escape the general law; it possesses, too, a theory of knowledge.[1]

But if a theory of that kind commands the general economy of the system connected with it, have we not committed a mistake in our method by leaving aside until the end of this book a study which, logically, ought to have been at the beginning ? No, we have not, for two reasons.

First, in Theosophy, as indeed in the majority of ancient

[1] The BHAGAVAD GITA constitutes the fundamental basis of this theory. The Bhagavad Gita is an episode inserted in the great Hindu épopée : MAHABHARATA.

philosophies, the theory of knowledge is largely deduced from the very principles of metaphysics. And that is not a contradiction. For a contradiction, those modern philosophers who, since Descartes, have forbidden man to look with confidence on the external world, would be more legitimately reproached. They have so well encaged the Thinker in himself, that, since then, he has never escaped. The first step of intelligence in its search for truth is to look round itself and to reason on the causes and ends of the Universe. That step already implies, in latency, a whole criteriology. Then, the thinker comes back to the " I," and tries to discover the inner mechanism which has allowed him to reach the conception of the world he professes. The theory of knowledge, wrapped in the folds of cosmology and theodicy, sets free its formula and condenses itself into formal doctrine. In such a way does Theosophy proceed: the structure of the Kosmos determines the structure of the thinking self. The one is explained by the other.

Secondly, the word " knowledge " has for Theosophists a special meaning. Under the infinite diversity of kosmic phenomena, a soul, a unique " self " vibrates and thrills. And the aim pursued by man, through and beyond the multiplicity of his reincarnations, is to become conscious of his identity with universal Consciousness. The cycle of evolution is achieved when this identity is realised. And it is realised by knowledge. From the moment when the monad, involuted on the lower planes of the Universe, thrills in answer to the first calls of the elemental essence[1] until the moment when the same monad reaches the extreme frontiers of the nirvanic planes, all human destiny gathers and expresses itself in that one watchword: to know. So that it is not a question of purely

[1] See above, p. 167.

platonic and purely intellectual research in Knowledge. It is the whole being of man which is in question. And when the whole being of man is in question, we find ourselves again at the centre, the focus of moral life. From the Theosophical point of view, " knowledge " is synonymous with " morality." And we could define it exactly : it is the totality of the means, the rules and the disciplines with the help of which the human Self ascends, little by little, to that state where duality solves itself in unity. Blissful state where man knows himself no more as SEPARATED from the rest of the world, but as IDENTICAL with it ![1]

That is why the theory of knowledge takes its place naturally at the end and not at the beginning of our work. We should have been unable to enter upon it if we had not already possessed the general lines and the spirit of the system.

* * *

Looked at from that standpoint, the history of knowledge includes two stages that we must distinguish with care. Man knows first by images, then he knows directly, or by intuition. We shall examine, one after the other, those two modes of knowledge.

First, the knowledge by images.

" The Knower," we are told, " does not know the things themselves in the earlier stages of his consciousness. He knows only the images produced in his vehicle by the action of the Not-Self on his responsive casing, the photographs of the external world."[2] Let us take care not to

[1] The reader should refer, in order to understand the present chapter, to the general description of human evolution given above (p. 49 seq.). Those pages are supposed known and we shall not come back to them again.

[2] A. Besant, *Thought Power, its Control and Culture*, p. 2. On the same question, consult, by the same author, *The Outward Court*,

imagine mind as a sort of mirror where the outer world is reflected. The operation is more complex: "The matter of the mind is actually shaped into a likeness of the object presented to it, and this likeness, in its turn, is reproduced by the Knower."[1] The organ of this reproduction is the mental body. But that mental body is not simple. It includes a fundamental element susceptible of combination with two distinct elements, which respectively constitute, united with it, two new bodies. The fundamental element is called MANAS. MANAS is "the reflection, in the atomic matter .... of the cognitional aspect of the Self."[2] Let us remember that the Self (the monad) can do nothing by itself. Its virtualities are manifested in matter and by matter. Consequently, the knowing principle is material. MANAS, wrapped up in finer matter, constitutes the causal body, subject of the abstract ideas; wrapped up in coarser matter, it constitutes the properly called mental, subject of the concrete ideas.[3] For the moment, we have nothing to do with the causal body; it is little developed in the majority at the present stage of evolution and "it remains unaffected by the mental activities directed to external objects."[4] After all, it is by the concrete mental that the monad is put in relation with the outer world. This is done, of course, by means of vibrations: "Each JIVA (by this word we mean the monad) .... becomes embodied, or clothed, in several garments of matter. As these garments of matter vibrate, they communicate

---

and *The Path of Discipleship*. Let us mention also a book published under the name of Revel (1905), *L'Evolution de la Vie et de la Conscience, du règne Animal aux règnes Humain et Surhumain.*

[1] *Thought Power*, p. 12.   [2] *Thought Power*, p. 25.

[3] These two kinds of matter are both borrowed from the mental plane.

[4] *Thought Power*, p. 26.

THEORY OF KNOWLEDGE

their vibrations to the matter surrounding them, such matter becoming the medium wherein the vibrations are carried outwards; and this medium, in turn, communicates the impulse of vibration to the enclosing garments of another JIVA, and thus sets that JIVA vibrating like the first. In this series of vibrations—beginning in one JIVA, made in the body that encircles it, sent on by the body to the medium around it, communicated by that to another body, and from that second body to the JIVA encircled by it—we have the chain of vibrations whereby one knows another."[1] And that is why knowledge is more than a simple image reflected in a mirror. Vibration emanated from a JIVA being a physical part of him, it is really something of himself which passes into the subject which receives the vibration.[2] Thought possesses, therefore, in as much as it is emitted, a sort of mechanical and material power which modifies mechanically its destination. We shall see presently the consequences of this Theosophical principle.

There is one we can consider immediately. The concrete mental is a source of illusion. It is so not only because it hides from the Self-Consciousness the thorough identity which conceals itself under the multiplicity of phenomena incessantly registered by it, but also because, left to itself, it registers unfaithfully, it deforms outer reality. In fact, " the mind is the result of past thinking, and is constantly being modified by present thinking....; each mind has its own rate of vibration, its own range of vibration, and it is in a state of perpetual motion, offering an everchanging series of pictures. Every impression

---

[1] *Thought Power*, p. 15-16.

[2] In the meantime, do not let us forget that thought is made of those same ELEMENTALS, which have, on their respective planes (causal, mental and astral) an autonomous existence. The emission of thought is like a discharge of elementals.

coming to us from outside is made on this already active sphere, and the mass of existing vibrations modifies and is modified by the new arrival. The resultant is not, therefore, an accurate reproduction of the new vibration, but a combination of it with the vibration already proceeding .... The influence of the mind as a medium by which the Knower views the eternal world is very similar to the influence of the coloured glass on the colours of objects seen through it. The Knower is as unconscious of this influence of the mind, as a man who has never seen, except through red or blue glasses, would be unconscious of the changes made by them in the colours of a landscape."[1]

So that the introduction of vibratory movement in the mechanism of knowledge confers on thought two distinct properties: THOUGHT POSSESSES A PHYSICAL POWER: IT IS A DEFORMER OF OUTER REALITY.

But we must add that all vibratory movement coming from outside does not necessarily produce in the receptive subject a thought in the real sense of the word. At the utmost it produces a sensation. To obtain thought, and, consequently, knowledge, the link must be perceived between the Thinking Self and the Not-Self. Sensation being given, the Self perceives it as coming from outside; he ascribes it to its exterior cause; then only does thought exist: "the perception of a Not-Self as the cause of certain sensations in the Self is the beginning of cognition."[2] Yet it is only the beginning of it. For, before the Self is able to establish the relation we are speaking of, the sensation must be repeatedly felt. The fixing element is the feeling of pleasure or pain which accompanies the sensation itself. By force of experiencing, through the

[1] *Thought Power*, p. 20-22, passim. [2] *Thought Power*, p. 49

THEORY OF KNOWLEDGE

same things, one or the other of these two impressions, the mind finally identifies the external object that causes it enjoyment or suffering. Then the link is established, " and that link is thought."[1]

" The observation, discrimination, reason, comparison, judgment "[2] form and develop by the same process. Pleasure and pain experienced, such are the agents, always at work, which bring man, by reflexion, to furnish, to organise his mentality, to classify the objects of his knowledge. Theosophical knowledge is essentially practical. And we were to expect it, for it is carried along, so to speak, by the stream of an intense moral dynamism.

And it is, moreover, from that moral point of view that occult science considers the education of the " thinker." Its " logic "—if we mean by this word the codification of the laws of human thought—is almost exclusively an asceticism, a treatise on Self-mastery.

In the course of the first stage of our evolutive ascension, we must live in "duality." A necessary stage, an inferior stage, too, so that we have every interest in crossing it as rapidly as possible, avoiding, as much as we can blunders, mistakes and useless steps. And if Theosophy concerns itself in defining the mechanism of knowledge " by images'" it is to show better to its adepts the snares to be avoided, the positive acts to be accomplished.

And again we see appearing the two great dangers which threaten the disciple at each turn of the path, the common cause of which is known to us : the deforming illusion and the blind power of thought.

THE DEFORMING ILLUSION comes from the fact that the vibrations received from outside affect a subject which is himself determined by a crowd of antecedent vibrations. This subject is not in a state of pure receptivity. He

[1] *Thought Power*, p. 45.   [2] *Thought Power*, p. 72.

amalgamates, he combines registered impressions, with his own mentality. His judgment deviates, commits numerous errors, does not appreciate good and evil as it ought to. The individual KARMA grows hea y with that onerous capital, and the progress is belated in proportion. " Very different would be our ideas of the world, if we could know it as it is, even in its phenomenal aspect, instead of by means of the vibrations modified by the mind."[1] As a remedy, " We should be continually trying to develop our receptive capacity."[2] But how? " The vibrations of the mind can be stilled, the consciousness being withdrawn from it ; an impact from without will then shape an image exactly corresponding to itself, the vibrations being identical in quality and quantity, uninterrupted by vibrations belonging to the observer."[3] Would it then be possible to check by a brake or a notch the perpetual mobility of our subjective vibrations? Yes: " Each man . . . . fixes the normal vibration-rate of his mind"[4] by the effort of his will, which applies the attention and obliges the mental to observe the object in itself and for itself.

To develop in him the sense of clear and precise observation, such is, for the adept in occult science, the means of escaping the peril of illusion.

But another peril, still more formidable, because it is more mysterious and more elusive, appears : it is THE PHYSICAL POWER OF THOUGHT. We live in a real atmosphere, laden with human vibrations. We emit a crowd of thoughts, and so do our neighbours. And all these

---

[1] *Thought Power*, p. 22. We have already said what is to be thought about the pretension, claimed by Theosophists, to base a moral system on evolutionism.
[2] *Thought Power*, p. 24.   [3] *Thought Power*, p. 23.
[4] *Thought Power*, p. 39.

THEORY OF KNOWLEDGE

thoughts exteriorize themselves without the knowledge of their producers. They furrow the world, like the swarming waves of millions of electric focuses. "All our thinkings cause vibrations in the mental body, that must, from the nature of things, be propagated through the surrounding mind-stuff."[1] So is explained the formation of what is called public opinion: "The strong thought of a great thinker goes out into the world of thought, and is caught up by receptive and responsive minds. They reproduce his vibrations and thus strengthen the thought-wave, affecting others who would have remained unresponsive to the original undulations. These, answering again, give added force to the waves, and they become still stronger, affecting large masses of people."[2] In the same way, there are "certain national ways of thinking, definite and deeply cut channels, resulting from the continual reproduction during centuries of similar thoughts, arising from the history, the struggles, the customs of a nation. These profoundly modify and colour all minds born into the nation, and everything that comes from outside the nation is changed by the national vibration-rate."[3] Therefrom come misunderstandings, conflicts, international shocks, murderous wars. All that comes from different ways of vibrating.

But what will the Theosophist do, amidst that formidable epidemic of vibratory vacilli? That is pre-eminently the practical question: "How much can I gain of good, and avoid of evil, seeing that I must live in a mixed atmosphere, wherein good and evil thoughts are ever active and are beating against my brain?"[4] Can I guard myself? Is a choice possible? And how am I to do it?

[1] *Thought Power*, p. 36. [2] *Thought Power*, p. 37.
[3] *Thought Power*, p. 37. [4] *Thought Power*, p. 38.

Let us reassure ourselves. The conscious adept in Theosophy is not the passive victim of these disquieting eddies. Between the two forces present—the mental which receives and the surroundings which vibrate—there is no parity. "Each man is the person who most constantly affects his own mental body. Others affect it occasionally, but he always." So, "his own influence over the composition of the mental body is far stronger than that of anyone else."[1] So that we can wait for the invasion with confidence. Yet on one condition : that we know how to oppose to it ceaselessly contrary thoughts: "If a man thinks truth, a lie cannot make a lodgment in his mind ; if he thinks love, hate cannot disturb him ; if he thinks wisdom, ignorance cannot paralyse him. Here alone is safety, here is real power."[2] Vigilance, such is the price of salvation. So the Theosophist, by knowledge, knows how to escape the double danger of illusion and of transmission of external thought. Certainly, he is not for all that exempt from following, like the others, the hard path of ordeal. But his mental, duly rectified by steady attention and by sound habits, is not mistaken about the nature of the pains and joys which are, for him, the criterion of good and evil. His joys are real joys and his sufferings are true sufferings. He does not mistake for joy what is, objectively, a cause of pain, nor for suffering what is objectively a cause of purer joy. He finds his way, amid the labyrinth of his own experience, with a more and more perfect security. And more rapidly than men plunged in the obscurity of ignorance, he walks, little by little, towards the state which characterizes the second mode of knowledge : intuition.

Before describing that second stage, let us try and judge the first. That criticism does not offer anything

[1] *Thought Power*, p. 39. [2] *Thought Power*, p. 39.

THEORY OF KNOWLEDGE

new. It is the strict application of the principles laid down in the previous chapters.

To bring back knowledge to a mere vibratory mechanism, is not to explain knowledge. It is, at the most, to account for a secondary aspect of the phenomenon. For the real problem is not to know how the subject who knows is physically impressed by the object known. It is to know how the passage, from the physical order to the special order that the philosophers call "intentional" order, comes about. One of my organs is affected by an impression, the cause of which is situated outside me. By what secret process is that physical impression changed into a sensation, later into an image, and finally into an idea, i.e., into objective, vital and conscious representations? All is there. And in vain will one multiply and reinforce the material vibrations, the mystery will not be solved at all. The strange power, that is attributed to thought by Theosophists, is a consequence of that fundamental error. That there exist cases of transmission of thought,[1] cases of telepathy give us the right to believe. But the mode of transmission is certainly not the one proposed to us by occult science. The thought, as such, does not "transmit" itself. It is a state of the subject who conceives, and does not exist out of him. If we wanted to push to its very end the Theosophical hypothesis, which attributes to the elemental essence, of which are made sensations and ideas, an independent life, we ought to admit that all transmitted thought is lost to whoever emits it. As soon as we identify the physical aspect of thought with its objective aspect, the inconvenience is unavoidable.

[1] A very vague term, and one which in no way presumes the real cause of these curious phenomena, about which we can only, at the present moment, stammer an explanation, subject to continuous revisions.

moment of its evolution, becomes able to construct "a mental image" of a higher order than that of a concrete object." The acquisition of that mental image, which is, really, a collective image, leads the Thinker towards the contemplation of the archetypal ideas which people the higher regions of the mental plane. Direct contemplation, without any intervening images, which, by its true name, is called INTUITION. What is the passage from mediate knowledge to intuitive knowledge: This is the point of the secret doctrine that we still have to elucidate.

The most important factor of that passage is CONCENTRATION: "In concentration, the consciousness is held to a single image; the whole attention of the Knower is fixed on a single point without wavering or swerving. The mind—which runs continually from one thing to another, attracted by external objects and shaping itself to each in swift succession—is checked, held in, and forced by the will to remain in one form, shaped to one image, disregarding all the impressions thrown upon it."[1] A painful exercise, and one which requires a display of "intense and regulated activity,"[2] chiefly at the beginning, since it is necessary, at the same time, to concentrate on one single image and to defend oneself against diversions. This double work risks dividing the attention and consequently weakening it. The ideal is reached, when inner pacification is realised: "Neither resistance nor non-resistance, but a steady quietude so strong that waves from outside will not produce any result, not even the secondary result of the consciousness of something to be resisted."[3]

The result of the concentration is not only to make precise to the minutest details, the knowledge of a given

[1] *Thought Power*, p. 79. [2] *Thought Power*, p. 80.
[3] *Thought Power*, p. 81.

THEORY OF KNOWLEDGE

object. It is also immediately to increase the effective force of the mental: " Steam allowed to expand in the air does not move a midge out of its path ; but along a pipe, the same steam would drive a piston."[1]

And further. While he is applying himself to concentrating and pacifying his mental, the Theosophist student makes a discovery. He feels himself " becoming conscious of a duality, of something which is controlled. The lower concrete mind is separated off[2] and the ' I '[3] is felt as of greater power, clearer vision, and there is involved a feeling that this ' I ' is not dependent on either body or mind. This is the first realisation, i.e., *feeling*, in consciousness, of the true immortal nature, already intellectually seen as existing."[4]

Now, " as the practice goes on, the horizon widens out, but as though inwards, not outwards, inwards and inwards continually, illimitably. There unfolds a power of knowing Truth at sight . . . . and intuition . . . . takes the place of reasoning."[5] One step more, and a deep transformation is going to be accomplished in the consciousness of the adept. To undergo it, it is necessary that, previously, the mental should have been maintained " in this attitude of fixed attention, *without the attention being directed to anything*. In this state the mental body shows

---

[1] *Thought Power*, p. 82.

[2] Separated from the " abstract mental," i.e., the causal body united with MANAS, the material reflection of the intellectual nature of the monad.

[3] Same observation as above (n. 2). The " I " in question herein constituted by the monad, manifested by MANAS, united to the causal body, this one being the permanent element which accompanies the individual through the whole series of his successive existences. Therefore, by becoming conscious of that " I," the Theosophist becomes conscious of his " immortality."

[4] That is to say, by mediate knowledge. See *Thought Power*, p. 83.

[5] *Thought Power*, p. 83-84.

no image ; its own material is there, held steady and firm,
receiving no impressions, in a condition of perfect calm,
like a waveless lake. This is not a state which can last
for more than a VERY BRIEF period, like the "critical
state" of the chemist, the point of contact between two
recognised and defined sub-states of matter. Otherwise
put, the consciousness, as the mental body, is stilled,
escapes from it, and passes into and out of the "laya
centre," the neutral point of contact between the mental
body and the causal body ; the passage is accompanied
by a momentary swoon, or loss of consciousness—the
inevitable result of the disappearance of objects of consciousness—followed by consciousness in the higher
order. The dropping out of objects of consciousness
belonging to the lower worlds is thus followed by the
appearance of objects of consciousness of a higher order.
Then can the Ego shape that mental body according to
his own lofty thoughts and permeate it with his own
vibrations. He can mould it after the high visions of the
planes beyond his own, that he has caught a glimpse of
in his own highest moments."[1] Blissful moments, during
which the adept, having transcended the world of forms,
is submitted no more to the limits of space, for "space
belongs to forms."[2] That adept becomes "conscious of
an object, say on another planet, not because his astral
vision acts telescopically, but because in the inner region
the whole Universe exists as a point ; such a man reaches
the Heart of Life, and sees all things therein."[3] "Anyone
who is conscious in the Self is conscious at all points of the
Universe." So is achieved the unfolding of that marvellous faculty, that intuition, which leaves far behind
the slow and inferior processes of reasoning. And if we
have quoted here, in spite of their length, the texts which

---

[1] *Thought Power*, p. 84-85. [2] *Thought Power*, p. 86.
[3] *Thought Power*, p. 87.

THEORY OF KNOWLEDGE 241

describe its birth and its progress, it is because they translate and condense the fundamental teaching of the Theosophical " mysticism " or " yoga."

"Mysticism," the practice of which is recognized as dangerous by the very people who recommend its use. A great physical exhaustion, acute headaches, obstinate inflammation of the brain, such are the dangers to which the student is habitually exposed.[1] And even if, by means of precautions and prudence, he were capable of avoiding them more or less, it would no doubt be thought that an asceticism which offered such inconveniences deserved to be severely judged as imposing on man acts contrary to nature. Is it not already a sign, external, it is true, but full of meaning, of the inanity of the doctrinal principles which pretend to justify it ?

Now, the veil of words being drawn aside, it is easy to denounce the weak points of all this strategy of the consciousness in its search for concentration, and in its quest of the teaching of that inner Self, wherein " the whole Universe is represented as a point."

And, first, we may do homage to Mrs. Besant for the cleverness with which she knows how to manage the passage from knowledge by images to intuitive knowledge : collection of the experiences by the mental body ; generalisation by the causal body ; fixed contemplation of a single object ; strengthening of mental power ; habit contracted little by little of discovering truth " at first sight " ; invention of the independent " Self " ; state of knowledge without object ; sudden trance followed by the direct vision of the Universe enclosed in the " self " : once more, all these stages are cleverly managed and graduated. In fact, they do not cause the solution of the problem to advance a single step. We do not know, we cannot know why and how, with a single bound, consciousness

[1] *Thought Power*, p. 102

passes from knowledge by images to intuitive knowledge. And we cannot know it, because this theory, apparently so minutely detailed, is based on an equivocation.

What exactly do they wish to imply by "intuitive knowledge"? Is it the kind of knowledge which excludes REASONING? Is it the kind of knowledge which excludes IMAGE? Between those two kinds of knowledge there is a wide gulf. I do not need to reason to understand that a thing is or is not, and that it cannot, simultaneously, and in the same relation, be and not be. I see it intuitively, and without being in the least obliged to use the deductive process. On the other hand, my senses put me in contact with an object. This contact is direct, immediate; it does not require image as an interpreter, although Theosophists say so, and in that sense too it can be called "intuitive." And it is in that sense that it differs absolutely from the other case. Indeed, when I pronounce the judgment of identity: "What is, is," I bring together, not two concrete realities, but two ideas, two concepts. In the second case, on the contrary, intuition bears on reality itself. In other words, there is an intuitive knowledge which is made by the intermediary of concepts or images, and an intuitive knowledge which bears directly on concrete things. But the first of these two intuitive knowledges does not necessarily include the second. And what is intuition "by images" or by conceptual substitution of reality EXCLUDES categorically what is intuition of the pure concrete reality. The equivocation, the sophism of Theosophy consists in mixing those two kinds of intuitive knowledge. Even if the causal body had developed infinitely, by concentration, the power of discovering truth "at first sight," it would not follow at all that this power could be transmuted, instantaneously, into the power of contemplating concrete reality without images or concepts. "The

THEORY OF KNOWLEDGE 243

state of knowledge without object " is not able to constitute the bridge that is supposed to be established between the two kinds of intuitive knowledge. That state simply creates a void that nothing can fill, or that can be filled only by other concepts, or by the subjective dreams of an organism over-excited and unsettled by the influence of a strange and morbid asceticism.[1]

But let us suppose that the event happens as Theosophists describe it. Here is the adept concentrated in himself : in his " Self," he discovers the Universe, and because he discovers the Universe included in that " Self," he is omnipresent, he is freed from the laws of space. It would be difficult to accumulate, in such a small number of words, a greater number of contradictory assertions.

If the adept finds the Universe in his " Self," it is apparently because the " Self " of the adept and the Universe are one. The " Self," in fact, is ATMA, the soul of the world. A critical situation, if ever there were one ! Ten, twenty, a thousand adepts will realise the same experience, and take consciousness of the same identity.[2]

[1] To say nothing of the confusion that Theosophy introduces here in the normal order of human knowledge. In fact, neither abstract nor concrete intuition is to be placed at the top, at the termination of knowledge, but at its beginning. We should be unable to acquire any science, if, on the one hand, we had not, when opening our mortal eyes, the intuition of concrete reality, and if, on the other hand, when opening the eyes of our mind, we had not the intuition of the first principles which are the basis of all judgment and reasoning.

Theosophy takes everything in reverse order : God is a resultant and not a cause ; in the same way idea (and what idea !) appears when human evolution is achieved !

[2] We multiply the number of adepts to make more apparent the absurdity of the reasoning. Really, the contradiction remains, be the number of adepts one or a thousand. For the question is, to know how an individual consciousness—which exists no more— can be conscious of the universal Self who has indrawn it.

They will therefore be conscious of being identical with one another, in the one soul which is the common foundation of their being. But, for them to be conscious of this deep identity, each of them must possess at least the sensation of being somebody, enjoying a separate consciousness, an autonomous Self. For none of them could be conscious of anything whatever if he could not bring back this consciousness to the individual Self which discerns, establishes and judges its own relation with the other Selfs. And here is the unavoidable dilemma. Either that individual consciousness is really identified with the universal soul, and in this case there remains no adept to be CONSCIOUS of the identity. Or the individual consciousness subsists, in which case, there is not identity but duality, and it is false to say that the adept discovers the Universe within his " Self."

These arguments are not dialectical play. They raise the question of the ultimate end and the supreme happiness of man. They compel the Theosophists to define exactly the goal to which we tend through our multiple reincarnations and by the progressive evolution of our mental and causal bodies. What is there at the end of the road ? The abolition or the permanence of the individual Self ? Will the happiness promised to me be mine ? Will it be the happiness of an immense Self, of which mine was only the pale and transitory projection on the planes of the " manifested " world ? Am I called to live a personal life, drinking from the infinite fountain of a Being distinct from myself ? Or is this Being so encroaching and jealous that he will not leave a particle of autonomy and of consciousness to those poor pilgrims who have been deceived by him, during millenia, with the illusion of possessing a right to immortality ?

Such is the true reach of the dilemma. Theosophists play fast and loose with it. They are wrong. For it is

THEORY OF KNOWLEDGE 245

not possible to play fast and loose with impunity with problems where uncertainty and scepticism have such serious consequences. In vain does Mrs. Besant say: " The nirvanic consciousness is the antithesis of annihilation; it is existence raised to a vividness and intensity inconceivable to those who know only the life of the senses and the mind."[1] Inconceivable intensity: be it so. But what does that existence matter to me if it is mine no more ? Such an existence is practically equivalent to annihilation. And when, in the same page, Mrs. Besant adds : " That Nirvana IS has been borne witness to in the past in the Scriptures of the world by those who enjoy it and live its glorious life,"[2] she passes from one pole of the dilemma to the other, and declares, in clear words, that the human Self and the soul of the world are not identical. And this is the ruin of all the pantheistic scaffolding, erected at great cost by Theosophists. Really it looks as if the authors of that system had trembled, at the moment of bringing forward the argument of their discourse, as trembled, in olden times, the disciples of Buddha, who taught, with the eternal fluidity of things, the annihilation of the ARHAT escaped from the wheel of the SAMSARA. And this is undoubtedly the reason why they hesitate to pronounce themselves clearly. They know very well that to our Western mentality, enlightened by the teachings of Christianity and of sound reason, the perspectives of the authentical NIRVANA will always remain inassimilable. So that they must surround with a halo of beauty the final episode of destiny, the beginning of which is marked by the awakening of " intuition." In fact, the halo is the brink of a bottomless pit. It evokes those marvellously decorated rooms which, in the Egyptian mastabas, overhang the subterranean galleries of

[1] *Ancient Wisdom*, p. 169.   [2] *Ancient Wisdom*, p. 169.

a tomb. It is the lintel of a door opened on the Unconscious.

After that, Theosophists may describe to us the advantages of a state which confers on the adept the privilege of omnipresence on all the points of the Universe. This privilege is a lure, under whatever aspect we regard it. If that " Self " discovered by intuition is identical with the soul of the world, it is not the " self " of the adept which is omnipresent, but the soul of the world, in which that fugitive " self " has been engulfed. And if that " self " of the adept keeps, while waiting for final reabsorption, a shadow of subsistence, it does not enjoy omnipresence any more because, being itself conditioned by a material coating, it is duly localised, as is matter, of which it remains a state. Only the pure spirit, separated from the mortal body, is freed from the laws of time and space. It is, in all the rigour of the term, OF ANOTHER WORLD. It is wherever its action is exercised, and distance does not exist any more for it. The spirit-matter of Theosophists could not don such properties.

So, one after the other, all the links of Theosophical " Knowledge " fall from the chain, and are shattered. The autonomous development of thought is an illusion which resolves itself into determinism. The hope of a conscious bliss is an illusion which resolves itself into the final annihilation of the individuality.

* * *

To close this long study, there only remains to formulate a few general conclusions. They will be brief ; for the reader, if he has followed us to the end, is himself able to deduce them.

We have applied, to the examination of the secret doctrine, a constant method : to bring back this doctrine to its fundamental principles. At first, the enterprise

THEORY OF KNOWLEDGE

seemed scarcely feasible. We had to deal with a forbidding system, encumbered with a strange terminology, placed under the authority of mysterious beings, armed with crushing anathemas against the profane who would dare to touch the treasure of a time-honoured and sacred tradition.

So, sometimes, in the burning heat of the desert at noon, citadels take shape on the horizon, with their bastions, their walls and their battlements. We come nearer. The castle vanishes. We have nothing in front of us, except perhaps a poor heap of sand changed into a mirror by the caprice of an over-heated atmosphere.

Under that imposing aspect, under that complicated vocabulary, under that haughty authoritativeness, Theosophy hides a groundwork of very simple ideas, which, as one can admit, do not bring any new element to the already too rich patrimony of human errors. A vague pantheism, a disconcerting materialism, a decayed evolutionism : such are the essential traits. The one soul of the world exteriorizes itself by means of a slow evolution, where reincarnation plays an episodical and subordinate part ; the whole history of the Universe is contained in that gesture, indefinitely, automatically repeated by the same anonymous and incognisable cause. Once more, all this is as old as the world, all this has repeatedly hurled itself against the categorical opposition of sound reason. Amidst the intellectual anarchy from which we suffer to-day, Theosophy presents a voice, a note, amongst other voices and other notes, and a note which seems, in fact, to come from very far off, and to come out of those hypogeums where sleep some of the great dreamers of ancient paganism.

What is new—and, is it really very new ?—is the pretension to apply to this foundation of old and false ideas a decoration, a varnish so well conceived that they constitute with it an indivisible whole. God, spirit, soul, freedom, justice, moral sacrifice, self-mastery, in a word, all these noble thoughts round which humanity, in spite of its blunders, loves to rally because it discovers in them, instinctively, the hall-mark of truth and idealism, seem to spring spontaneously from the bosom of a system which, BY ESSENCE, eliminates and ignores them.

And there reside, together, the allurement exercised by occult science, and, we dare add it, the scruple of the critic who has to give a sound judgment on it. This critic, if he is a Catholic, will certainly have no difficulty in discerning that between Christian faith and Theosophical faith, there is no common measure. He will say so without hesitation. And, by saying it, he will accomplish a work of beneficence. And one would not be justified in reproaching him for that work, even from the standpoint of mere human fairness. In India, it is said, the true disciples of the Brahmans do the same : they refuse to listen to a theory which distorts their beliefs.

And yet the critic owes it to himself not to violate, under the pretext of denouncing the error, the laws of impartiality. Now, he finds himself struggling with an elusive doctrine, where, at every moment, words come into conflict which exclude each other, when taken in their real meaning. Theosophy is pantheistic, and it speaks of God as of a personal being, distinct from his creatures. Theosophy is determinist, and it strikes up hymns to freedom. Theosophy conceives man as composed of material coatings, and it chants the beauty of intelligence, the splendours of the spirit. Theosophy terminates destiny with a plunge into unconsciousness, and it describes the magnificence of a bliss which reminds us of the Christian heaven : union with God in knowledge, love, and fulness of being . . . . How will one be able to steer through this contradictory chaos ? And will

THEORY OF KNOWLEDGE

not the critic incur the reproach of injustice and incomprehension if he neglects deliberately some aspects of Theosophy which can, after all—how many times has it not been repeated?—wrench souls from their earthly preoccupations, and open to them the vast horizons of a life nobler and more worth living? Has not Christ forbidden us to break a bruised reed, and to quench smoking flax?

There is only one way of solving that captious objection. It is evident that Theosophy juxtaposes irreconcilable notions. The question is, then, to know which are, amongst those notions, those which constitute the fundamental structure of the doctrine. Now, it is impossible, on that capital point, to go on with an equivocation: we have, with the help of texts, characterised and defined the principles of the secret doctrine, the frames which uphold the whole building. The rest, whether one wishes it or not, is an excrescence which is added from outside, and does not justify itself by any valuable proof or reasoning. Logically, pantheism leads to the negation of a God infinite in his being and in his power, and to the negation of human personality. Logically, the materialistic origin of vibratory whirls leads to the negation and destruction of religious life. We ask it: under the pretext of not breaking a bruised reed, and of not quenching smoking flax, is it prudent to let souls in good faith enter in the wake of a theory which leads, can we contradict it, to such nefarious consequences? And do we not live at a time when, precisely, the most urgent task which imposes itself on the attention of thoughtful men, is the task which consists in attaching to sure principles the flotsam of morality and of spirituality which float on the ocean of modern materialism? In the Theosophical system, morality, freedom, and idealism are and will always remain flotsam, all the more exposed to sinking because they are hurled against the rock of a teaching which incessantly contradicts them. And it is, too, a work of purification to say to the souls who are attracted and seduced by the external, superficial and incoherent aspect of the Theosophical doctrine that their good faith has been deceived.

And if we had, in a final analysis, to characterise the thought we have just studied, we should define it as : *A doctrine which, after having expelled, by virtue of its principles, all the notions which constitute the time-honoured capital of human morality and intelligence, re-introduces the same notions as contraband, and without troubling to find out whether they have their place in a system which excludes them.* It is no wonder, then, that many minds, badly informed, are deceived, and perhaps, after all, Theosophists are themselves the dupes of their own credulity. As F. Lacordaire has said : " A sincere love of good can be allied to a false wisdom, and a false wisdom can deceive eminent hearts even to the point of exaltation."